An African Treasure

In search of Gladys Casely-Hayford 1904-1950

Yema Lucilda Hunter

Sierra Leonean Writers Series

African Treasure
In search of Gladys Casely-Hayford 1904-1950

© Yema Lucilda Hunter 2015

1st Edition
Yema Lucilda Hunter: 978-9988-1-1134-7
Layout Design & Publishing:
P.D. Casely-Hayford
www.laterallycreative.com

2nd Revised Edition
SLWS: 978-99910-54-57-5

Cover Design: Colleone www.colleone.com

For Kobina, who lost his mother much too soon, and in
whom I recognise
So many of her best qualities.

And for
Jessie and Mark,
who never knew this grandmother

Yema Lucilda Hunter

To God Be the Glory

Acknowledgements

I am indebted to Dr. Adelaide M. Cromwell for graciously allowing me to use some of the material she collected for her biography of Adelaide Casely-Hayford, to my cousin-in- law Pauline Casely-Hayford for doing such a beautiful job with the layout design and publishing for the 1ˢᵗ edition, and to my son, Mark Hunter for his gorgeous new cover design.

Special thanks go to Osa Barima Kwesi Attah, Chief of Cape Coast, and Mr. Nokoe, unofficial historian of Axim, for their kindness and assistance. I am also grateful to my steadfast friends Daphne Pratt and the late Nance Mjamtu-Sie for their help with research in Freetown, my sister Smita Caulker-Tomalin for her useful comments on the manuscript and my sister, Velma Caulker-Mitchell, who did the copy-editing.

I am also most grateful to the archivist and archival assistant at the National Archives in Freetown, Sierra Leone, and to staff members of the Africana Section of the Balme Library, University of Legon, the George Padmore Library and Public Records and Archives Administration Department, all in Accra, Ghana, Jean Shaw, my niece, Ngadi Kponou, and my daughter, Jessie Logan, who helped me access Gladys's publication Take Um So at the British Library in London. Finally, to my husband, Kobina Hunter, I say thanks for everything.

Introduction

My main purpose in attempting this biography was to leave for my children an account of the life of Gladys Casely-Hayford, their paternal grandmother whom they never knew. She died in the Gold Coast (now Ghana) in August, 1950.

A month or so after her death, *The Sierra Leone Daily Mail* carried this announcement:

'Under the auspices of a committee representative of the many friends of Gladys Casely-Hayford who recently died at Accra, Gold Coast, a memorial service will be held at Wesley Church, Trelawney Street on Sunday 24th September at 3.30 p.m.

An augmented choir will lead the singing and the address will be delivered by the Rev. G.L. Leopold, M.A. ... All friends and admirers of this illustrious lady are kindly invited to attend the service'.[1]

Also, in a book about Sierra Leone published about four years later, Roy Lewis, a British social historian, described her as 'outstanding among Creole literati'.[2] Yet Gladys Casely-Hayford has hardly been mentioned as a personality of note since Sierra Leone became independent, and then only by one or two academics and those, now aged, members of the Freetown community who derived a great deal of pleasure in the 1930s and 40s from her variety shows, musical plays, poetry readings and retellings of West African folk tales.

Perhaps this state of affairs is not all that surprising, since a lot of her work has been lost and only a few of her poems ever appeared in print in her lifetime. However, outside Sierra Leone, especially in the United States, a certain amount of interest in her poetry has been shown in recent years, and some of her published work has appeared in anthologies. In fact, my secondary purpose in writing this book was to set the record straight once and for all after discovering that in some literary circles in America, Gladys Casely-Hayford is wrongly thought to have been an African-American, or perhaps an African who migrated to the United States and was part of the Harlem Renaissance of the 1920s.[3] My research has uncovered no evidence that she ever even visited the United States, though she once left home to go there.

When I embarked on the project, almost sixty years had passed since her death, with only a few of her contemporary friends and relations still alive. Other sources of information were equally scanty, though invaluable, namely, *Memoirs* and the brief *Profile of Gladys* written by her mother, Adelaide Casely-Hayford, some letters from Adelaide Casely-Hayford to Gladys's father quoted in Adelaide Cromwell's biographical work, *An African-Victorian Feminist: the life and times of Adelaide Smith Casely Hayford 1868-1960*, and many letters from both Adelaide and Gladys Casely-Hayford to Anna Melissa Graves who, with useful notes, included them in her book, *Benvenuto Cellini had no prejudice against bronze: letters from West Africans*.

Gladys's letters to Anna Graves are so revealing that I deeply regretted not being able to lay hands on any others she must have written in her lifetime, especially to her father, mother and brother. However, conversations with the few people I was able to interview, the documentary sources at my disposal, as well as unpublished collections of poems, song lyrics and retellings of West African folk tales in the possession of her son, Kobina Hunter, gave me considerable insight into her personality, attitudes and aspirations. But I certainly do not presume to have found out all there is to know about her, hence my decision to call the work a 'search'. Another interested person might in future be able to throw more light on the life of this extraordinary woman, especially on those periods she spent in the Gold Coast about which my research turned up very little.

I hope, though, that I have provided enough information to show that Gladys Casely-Hayford was much more than just 'the child of a famous mother'* – and father too, for that matter. Her father was the Honourable Joseph Ephraim Casely Hayford, of the Gold Coast, a member of the colony's Legislative Council, a political activist, philosopher, nationalist and pan-Africanist, successful barrister, journalist, newspaper editor, and one of the first black Africans to write a novel in English.[4] Like Gladys's mother, he was distinguished enough in his day to be honoured with the award of an MBE** by the British colonial government.

Gladys once told one of my informants that it was very hard to be the child of a famous mother.

**Member of the Most Excellent Order of the British Empire*

Chapter One

Family background and the early years

AMONG the Creoles[1] of Freetown, Sierra Leone, Adelaide Casely-Hayford, Gladys's mother, belonged to that select group known somewhat disapprovingly as 'aristos'. What separated 'aristos' from the rest of the African population of Freetown was that they normally spoke English, even among themselves, and that they behaved more like the British colonisers than their fellow Africans in the food they habitually ate, the clothes they habitually wore and their standards of etiquette.

Adelaide Casely-Hayford was outstanding among them. In the 1920s and 30s her name often appeared in the local papers, either in connection with the school she founded, or with her articles and speeches on social matters, including the education of African girls and Christian marriage. Excerpts from her memoirs were published in the now defunct *West African Review* in the early 1950s, and she also published two short stories of which the better known, *Mista Courifer* appeared in a well known American anthology.[2] She was one of the regulars on the colonial Governor's guest list.

Her own mother whose maiden name was Anne Spilsbury, came from a wealthy merchant family, though that wealth seems largely to have disappeared during Adelaide's early childhood. Anne Spilsbury became the second wife of William Smith junior, who was the product of the senior Smith's union with the daughter of a Fante chief in the Gold Coast.

William Smith senior was English and first came to West Africa as young man working for the Royal African Company.[3] Years later, he became a Commissary Judge at the Courts of Mixed Commission set up in Freetown after the abolition of the

Slave Trade to adjudicate in cases involving captured slave-ships. Aged seventeen, William Smith junior, accompanied his father to Freetown, and also became associated with the Courts of Mixed Commission, first as a humble clerk, but later as a Registrar of the Courts. He held that position from 1850 till 1872 when he retired. That same year, he moved with his wife, and their seven children first to England, then, on account of his wife's delicate health, to the British Island of Jersey which enjoyed a milder climate. Adelaide was only four years old when the family emigrated and grew up entirely in Europe. She was a foundation pupil of the Jersey Ladies' College in St. Helier, the main town on the island, and later studied music at a branch of the Stuttgart Conservatory in Germany.

Mrs. Anne Smith died when Adelaide was only seven; her father, when she was twenty-seven and still unmarried. She and her middle sister, Emma, who was also unmarried, fulfilled their father's dying wish by returning to their relations in Africa; but after so many years away, they felt like misfits in Freetown and frequently returned to England on visits. It was on one such visit in 1903 that Adelaide,

'...received a letter from a lawyer from the Gold Coast, who was spending some months in England. It was a very short letter, voicing the request that he might be allowed to meet me. He said that he had tried unsuccessfully, through several mutual friends, to bring this about, so he was taking the bull by the horns and wanted to know whether he would be permitted to call.' [4]

Having agreed to meet the lawyer from the Gold Coast, Adelaide was,

'very much impressed by Joseph Ephraim Casely Hayford's quiet, unassuming, straight-forward demeanour'. [5]

Usually referred to as 'J.E. Casely Hayford', her suitor has been described elsewhere as 'a dapper man of medium height, with a charming personality and keen sense of humour.'[6] He was also a devout Christian, which must have added to his appeal, for Adelaide Smith was a young woman of strong religious convictions.

J.E.Casely Hayford's lineage and education made him one of the Fante élite comprising a number of intellectuals and professionals as well as a wealthy merchant class living in and around the coastal town of Cape Coast. He was one of the four sons of the Reverend Joseph de Graft Hayford and his wife, Mary Awuraba, a member of an equally prominent family – the Brews.[7]

After they became better acquainted, he told Adelaide hat his adored first wife had died in childbirth two years earlier, leaving him with a five-year-old son, Archie, who badly needed a mother. Adelaide confessed that she also had only a second-best affection to offer, since the love of her life had died of tuberculosis four years earlier. She, however, quickly agreed to marry the charming Gold Coaster, deciding that they could make a good life together in a marriage that would be, 'based on the solid foundation of mutual understanding, comradeship, tolerance and good will.'[8]

Had Mr. Casely Hayford not been a member of the Cape Coast élite, it is highly unlikely that Adelaide Smith would have agreed to marry him, for her own biographer quoted an informant as saying, though in another context, that as a result of her upbringing, she firmly believed that only the upper classes should mingle. [9] This informant gains credence from Mrs. Casely-Hayford's own words in her memoirs where she confesses to being 'something of a snob.'[10]

She married J.E.Casely Hayford in Shepherd's Bush, London, on September 10, 1903; and in November of the same year, the couple set sail for the Gold Coast. Mr. Casely Hayford had a flourishing legal practice in Axim, at the time a bustling port several miles west of Cape Coast.[11] He had his chambers on the ground floor of an imposing two-storey house overlooking Axim harbour. The upper storey which they shared with his widowed mother was surrounded by a verandah nine feet wide.

On May 11, 1904, a daughter they christened Gladys May, was born to the Casely-Hayfords – prematurely and with an unfortunate abnormality in her left hip. Another of Dr. Cromwell's informants told her that a doctor had attributed Gladys's defective hip joint to a fright her mother received while she was pregnant – perhaps the same one mentioned in Mrs. Casely-Hayford's memoirs – when a chimpanzee suddenly appeared a few yards away from where she lay half dozing on the verandah. This explanation sounds pretty far-fetched to the modern reader, however. Since she also mentions in her memoirs that Gladys's arrival nearly killed her, it is quite possible that the defect was the result of a birth injury. Mrs. Casely-Hayford, a small and dainty woman, was having her first child at the age of thirty-six and under what must have been, in 1904, primitive conditions.

As a result of the hip defect, Gladys's left leg was slightly shorter than the other, and with little muscular development, which made learning to walk difficult. Before she was two years old, her parents therefore decided that she should be seen by a specialist in London, and Mrs. Casely-Hayford traveled to England with the two children. Her husband was supposed to join them there a few weeks later, but for some reason, that never happened. In her reply to one of his letters Mrs. Casely-Hayford sounds rather wistful in parts, giving the reader the impression that she might have been wondering whether, despite the expense of keeping two households going, her husband preferred to have his family living overseas while he got on with his increasingly busy life. [12]

Apparently, the English weather did not suit Gladys's constitution. In one letter, Mrs. Casely-Hayford writes to tell her husband that the little girl, whom she always refers to as 'Baby', has had such a heavy cold that she has had to confine her to one room with a fire night and day. [13] But Gladys was also developing satisfactorily. Her mother was delighted that even at that early age, she already had 'a wonderful grasp of English', and told her husband that while she was writing to him, Gladys handed her a scrap of pink paper which she said was a letter to her father, asking that it be enclosed with her mother's. [14] On another occasion, Mrs. Casely-Hayford reports that as soon as she told Gladys that she wanted to teach her a new prayer, she put her little hands together and said, 'My dear Papa, I hope you are well for Christ's sake, Amen.'[15]

As far as her behaviour was concerned, Gladys seems to have been no trouble whatsoever, always sitting quietly opposite her mother while she dealt with her correspondence. In another letter, Mrs. Casely-Hayford mentions an occasion when Gladys had to spend two nights with her younger sister, Mrs. Annette Easmon, and seemed quite unperturbed when she awoke to find someone other than her mother lying beside her.

They returned to the Gold Coast on doctor's advice because, after that bad cold, Gladys went on to contract 'every conceivable bronchial ailment.' [16] In their absence, Mr Casely Hayford had moved inland to Tarkwa, a gold mining centre and railway town in the south western part of the Gold Coast where they later joined him. Mrs. Casely-Hayford found Tarkwa an extremely dreary place.

> 'There was no food except mutton and coco-yams, and malnutrition made the children break out in terrible sores all over their bodies. It made me weep to dress them... The house itself was a wretched affair, built of wood with concrete partitions inside, and with barbed wire at the windows to keep out thieves. Often as we sat at our evening meal, rats danced their minuets right above the table till I was almost distracted with fright. The worst aspect of my

life…was the lack of companionship. One educated woman came to spend a few days in the place, but otherwise, I was entirely surrounded by illiterate peasants.'[17]

Small wonder then that, on finding herself pregnant again, the memory of that first traumatic experience of childbirth made her decide to return to her sisters in London for what she expected to be another ordeal.

Her husband had booked a first-class cabin for them on a German boat, but when the Chief Steward discovered that, despite her English name Mrs. Casely-Hayford was an African, he cancelled that accommodation and put her and little Gladys in what, in her opinion, must have been,

'…the worst second-class cabin on the boat. There was no stewardess, no bell and no sofa for Gladys. In my pregnant condition, I could not climb up to the top bunk and dared not put Gladys there; so we had to share the same narrow lower bunk and she kicked me all night.' [18]

Being remarkably self-confident as well as fluent in German, Mrs. Casely Hayford refused to accept the Chief Steward's decision and confronted the ship's captain on his private deck about their situation. Her determination paid off; for on the captain's orders, their accommodation was grudgingly changed to a somewhat more comfortable cabin. However, she went into labour prematurely during the voyage; thus her second experience of childbirth proved to be as much of an ordeal as the first and, sadly, this time unrewarding. Assisted by the ship's doctor and barber, after several hours of suffering, she finally gave birth to a stillborn baby. Gladys remained her only child.

It is unclear why Mrs. Casely-Hayford did not return to the Gold Coast as soon as she had recovered. In her memoirs, she implies that she had some family obligations – one sister, Mrs.

Easmon, who had been a widow since 1900, had recently undergone major surgery and could only do light work. Another sister, Emma was not robust enough to bear the burden of looking after the entire household which included Mrs. Easmon's two young children, Charles and Kathleen. Being highly intelligent, Mrs. Casely-Hayford may also have begun to realise even before she left the Gold Coast for the second time that though they had remained intimate enough to conceive another child, her marriage was no longer the calmly affectionate union she had envisaged.

Whatever the true reason for the delay, she was certainly in no hurry to go back to the Gold Coast, for she put Gladys in a nearby kindergarten, rented an unfurnished four-roomed apartment in the same building near Notting Hill where her sisters lived, and acquired some lodgers to help with the expenses. In her spare time she became busy with charity work and church meetings, even venturing to do some public speaking. She mentions in her memoirs that she very much disliked living apart from her husband, but given the full life she was leading in England, one cannot help wondering whether it might not have been the social disadvantages of his absence that she truly disliked. Perhaps it was that, together with concern for Gladys's health (the doctor thought she might be developing tuberculosis) that made her finally return to the Gold Coast.

During her absence, Mr. Casely Hayford had moved his practice yet again – this time to Sekondi, another harbour town some miles west of Cape Coast but not as far away as Axim. For some reason, he now decided to settle his family in Cape Coast while he continued living where he worked. This arrangement may have suited Mrs. Casely-Hayford quite nicely at first, because Cape Coast, which had been the capital of the Gold Coast till 1877, was a much larger, more developed town than Tarkwa. It was also a more congenial place in which to live as there were other women of her education and class in the community. Being an excellent pianist, she must have been delighted to be able to borrow a piano. She went on to form a social club with other women and they met once a week for music and games. However, though Sekondi was not all that far away, she saw so little of her husband that she soon came to the conclusion that she would be happier in her own country.

In her memoirs, she does not elaborate on the reasons why her marriage completely fell apart. However, her two long absences from the Gold Coast after 1906 probably played a part in the couple's estrangement, as well as Adelaide's independent, even feminist personality. It is also quite likely that she discovered her husband had another wife under customary law. This possibility is strongly supported by information provided in Dr Cromwell's biography of her. In it she cites Mr. Casely Hayford's will which, apart from major bequests to his son, Archie, and the bequest of a house to Gladys, mentioned a Princess Ambah Saah, of Lower Wassaw and two other daughters, Awura Abba and Awura Amba, even before mentioning his wife.[19] If Mr. Casely Hayford did have a second family, Mrs. Casely-Hayford with her European background, outspokenness and strict Christian values would neither have found that situation tolerable nor endured it in silence for long. As she succinctly puts it in her memoirs,

> '…things came to such a climax that we drew up a Separation Agreement and I decided to return to Freetown'. [20]

What little is known of Gladys's life during this period is in her mother's short article about her:

> 'She was a lonely little girl and I fully realized how inadequate I was as a playmate. When we played 'follow my leader,' she was disgusted with my leadership and would ask whether she might not take my place. Sometimes with her spade and bucket, we would go down to the seashore together and she

would watch with envious eyes some practically naked little boys with whom she longed to play. When I allowed her to do so, keeping an eye on them all the time, it did make her so happy. In her childhood days in England she found great solace in her imaginary friend, Peggy, whom we were admonished to treat with the utmost respect. When riding a bus, we were cautioned not to sit on Peggy and to allow her plenty of breathing space, much to the amazement of other passengers.

She didn't like textbooks and hated arithmetic; but she was a voracious little reader, devouring Kingsley's 'Heroes' from cover to cover at the age of seven. I tried to teach her, but not very successfully. Some ideas stuck in her brain, however, because one evening we were watching a beautiful sunset and she said, 'Oh, mother, do look at that lovely archipelago in the sky.' [21]

During the year or so they spent in England on that second occasion, Gladys had forgotten the little Fante she had picked up; but on their return home, she quickly become fluent in the language and acted as her mother's interpreter when necessary. From Mrs. Casely-Hayford's account, she seems to have been a well-behaved, highly intelligent, imaginative and sociable little girl who must have felt that loneliness keenly.

---OOOIIIOOO---

Gladys and her mother arrive in Freetown in May, 1914. Their first home is with her cousin, Charles Easmon, who has just joined the government service as a physician. Still a bachelor, Dr. Easmon must have been delighted when his 'Auntie Addie' offered to keep house for him. The arrangement lasted until later that year when the First World War broke out and he was drafted to the Cameroons as a military surgeon. The Casely-Hayfords then moved to a small, two-storey house in the heart of Freetown, somewhere along Oxford (now Light-Foot Boston) Street. Gladys's son, Kobina, remembers his grandmother telling him that a ghost haunted their home and that, to keep the phantom at bay, she opened Bibles at Psalm 23 and put them on the floor at the entrance to their bedrooms.

Though she was receiving a small allowance as part of her Separation Arrangement, Mrs. Casely-Hayford put her considerable energy and talents to good use, including earning extra money by teaching music part-time at the Annie Walsh Memorial School.[22] Gladys, who was now almost eleven, attended the same school.[23] Her remarkable command of English seems to have impressed her teachers, for in a letter to her husband, Mrs. Casely-Hayford reports that the headmistress told her that had Gladys been an English girl in England, she would have made a splendid journalist.[24]

I discovered little else about Gladys's life at this age but again, from her mother's memoirs and profile of her, learned more about her character. During her life-time Mrs. Casely-Hayford fell seriously ill several times, though she lived to be ninety-one. On such occasions she says young Gladys nursed her 'with a wisdom and foresight quite beyond her years'.[25] As shown in the following incident described by her mother, Gladys was also a remarkably courageous girl, especially for one so imaginative:

'One night she woke up from a sound sleep when I called her before lapsing into unconsciousness which was to last till four o'clock the next afternoon. The neighbours heard Gladys's cries and rushed in, but she felt that she must call my friend, Mrs. Rice, to come to my assistance. It must have been about midnight, but in her thin night-gown, she ran out, passing the giant cotton-tree, about which there were so many weird tales. She found Mrs. Rice and her household deep in slumber, but with great determination, kept on throwing gravel at the bedroom windows, till at last it had the desired effect.' [26]

Aged fifteen, Gladys again has to nurse her mother through a serious illness. This time it is an attack of 'Spanish Flu'—the deadly pandemic sweeping across the world after the First World War. Without the assistance of any doctor or nurse, since so many people are fighting for the lives of others or their own, Gladys helps her mother survive by using 'her own God-given intuition and common sense.'[27]

As she enters adolescence, Gladys starts writing poetry. It is extremely frustrating that very few of the poems in her unpublished collection give any indication of when she wrote them. However, we do have a record of one of her earliest poems, which, according to her own annotation, she wrote at the age of twelve or thirteen:

My Second Poem

Just a tiny rippling wavelet dancing to the shore,
Just a bushy squirrel cracking brown nuts, from its store.

Just the twitter of a sparrow in the bower eaves,
Just a duet twixt the night wind and the falling leaves.

Just some tiny dewdrops glistening on the blades of grass.
Just a nearly-sleeping daisy nodding as I pass,
Just the prayers of humble hearts ascending from the sod,
Giving thanks for love and mercy, lying down with God.

Mrs. Casely-Hayford soon decided that her gifted daughter ought to benefit from a British education rather than remain at the Annie Walsh Memorial School. Reading through the forthright letter she wrote to her husband in December 1918, I suspect that she had raised the subject of Gladys's education time and time again with rising frustration at his failure to take up her concern. In that letter she tells him that, having heard from well informed sources that the legal business is thriving in the Gold Coast, she wants to know what plans he has for Gladys's education; that it would be more convenient for her to live with her sister (now resident in Sierra Leone, Mrs. Easmon was apparently thinking of going to live with her son who was stationed in a town about seventy-five miles away from Freetown), but she does not want to make Gladys a boarder because she is afraid of the bad influence of other girls as well as the harmful effects of the poor boarding home food. She urges her husband not to allow any grudge he may hold against her to cause their child to suffer, especially since Gladys has talents which need to be nurtured. That would be most unfair, she tells him, and something he will live to regret.[28]

The exchange of correspondence between Gladys's parents on the subject of her education seems to have lasted throughout 1919, with her father apparently agreeing to send her to England but never providing the wherewithal for her passage, tuition fees and accommodation. Not having had the privilege of reading more of these letters myself, I was grateful to have Dr. Cromwell's assessment of the situation. In her opinion, Mrs. Casely-Hayford might have felt her husband was not as interested in furthering the education of a girl child, hence her rising annoyance – and that there might also have been additional resentment over how much he was spending on his son, Archie, who was by this time a student at Cambridge University in England.[29]

Gladys seems to have spent Christmas of 1919 with her father and brother in the Gold Coast and, since Mr. Casely Hayford had neither seen nor had a conversation with her for more than five years, that visit might well have been what, in the end, made him take the necessary steps towards sending her overseas. In any case, on January 19, 1920, his wife is able to write thanking him for the long awaited funds. She is so pleased at the successful outcome of the pressure she has put on him that she signs off the letter, 'Yours with love, Adelaide Casely Hayford'[30] instead of the formal 'Yours sincerely' or 'Yours very sincerely' she more often uses when writing to him after their separation.

Chapter Two

Life Unfolding

SHORTLY after returning to Freetown from her Christmas visit to the Gold Coast, Gladys leaves home to attend a boarding school in Wales called Penrhos College. The headmistress, a Miss Rose Tovey, had been her mother's friend at the Jersey Ladies' College. I have unearthed no information about how well Gladys coped with her studies, except that Miss Tovey once wrote to tell Mrs. Casely-Hayford that she had been extremely impressed by her poem Ears. Miss Tovey considered it 'the finest ever written by a Penrhos girl.'[1]

Ears

When God made the world and all therein,
In a sad moment of great wistfulness
And loneliness, He fashioned Him a man.

"That he may cling," God said –and shaped his hands.

"That he may laugh," God said – and made his mouth,

Then paused debating, whether vision given
Would make the creature infinitely wise:

"That he may see, God said – and shaped his eyes;
"That he may follow Me, until I choose that we
shall meet,"

God said – and gave the creature feet.

The finished creature, now with life imbued,

On the world's threshold palpitating stood;
Whilst suns, stars, worlds, and moons about
him whirled,

The full creation, pulsing still being hurled
Into position by God's mighty Hand;

The cooling sea revolving the hot land.

Man started forward. "Turn to me,"God cried;
But man, who heard not, could not turn aside,

Walked swiftly into life, bereft of fears.
God caught him back, and laughing
Made him ears.

From the heart of conscience,
The path of silence,
The thunder of chaos,
The cycle of years,
The mystery of singing,
The whisper of angels,
The devil's shadow
God made the ears,
Then laughing at this modeled piece of grace
Shaped question-wise and wondering what use
Mortals would make of them,
He kissed the ears in place.

With no other letters at my disposal, I have also discovered
nothing about how well Gladys adjusted to boarding school and
life away from home, but she might have been unhappy at

Penrhos College because, by December 1920, it seems her father has arranged for her to go to another school called Copeland in or near the English seaside town of Brighton.[2] According to Mrs. Casely-Hayford, the arrangement was made without her knowledge or consent, so it is possible it was Gladys herself who persuaded Mr. Casely-Hayford to arrange the transfer. Her mother felt even more resentful about the change of school because she feared Copeland might be a private finishing school— the kind of institution in whose educational standards she had no confidence whatsoever. In a letter to her husband dated December 17, 1920, she tells him that she has a horror of such schools because they usually turn out girls with nothing but a smattering of knowledge on any subject whereas Gladys deserves much better. She, however, seems to have come to appreciate the school later. In another letter to her husband,[3] she expresses gratitude for the opportunities Gladys is getting and hopes that she can continue to benefit from them for at least another three years.

Mrs. Casely-Hayford would certainly have started teaching music and the piano early in life to any child of hers; but since I have found no evidence that Gladys studied music anywhere else, it was probably at Copeland that she had the opportunity to advance her technical knowledge of music and master the piano, hence her mother's satisfaction with the school. Gladys became an accomplished musician who not only played the piano exceptionally well, but also composed many songs and dance tunes. *African Nights* and another of her songs, *Dance this Waltz with Me* were published by Cecil Lenox Ltd of 132 Charing Cross Raod, London in 1927.

African Nights

African nights, African nights, how you are calling me.
Blue waves beating golden sand, shade 'neath the palm tree,

And drifting wide upon the tide
Boat songs from the canoe;
Beautiful African nights, I'm coming home to you.

I'm always crying, always sighing for the April rain,
I'm always sighing, always crying for my home again.
African nights, African nights, etc.

During that period Gladys writes several other poems,
including one composed beside the grave of her godfather, the
Anglo-Sierra Leonean composer, Samuel Coleridge Taylor.[4]

Music

Music dwells everywhere.
With rose leaves, falling in a gentle flutter,
And in the sweetest word, that baby lips may utter,
In 'Mother' there's music.

Music dwells everywhere.
By the young brook, that on its way hath sped,
Music oft lays to rest, her weary head.
In wildest wave, there's music.

Music dwells everywhere.
Thus can you wonder, if my spirit long
To seek out music's offspring – gentle song?
In all the world there's music.

* Written at the grave of Coleridge Taylor at fifteen.

Aged sixteen, she writes, the quaint and lilting:

'Jenny's birthday'

Oh! I must up so early,
And hie me through the corn,
To pluck some four-leaved clovers,
For 'tis Jenny's birthday morn.
They must be pulled when shining,
All glistening with wild dew;
Or else, the spell won't work at all,
Nor Jenny's luck come true.

Then I must home to Luber,
And bid him leave his sheep,
To come and wish my love good morn
And healthy rise from sleep.
Else Jenny'd take to weeping,
I really can't see why;
But if she weeps on day of birth,
Why – all the year she'll cry!

And the rather solemn:

'A Harper's Prayer'

Give me the strength to sweep across the strings,
So that the hall, with its full cadence rings:
Give me the power to make emotions rise,
And thrill the souls, until they seek the skies.
Give me the knowledge of the hearts I tune,
So that I may not weave my spell too soon:
Above all, give me gentleness, to lull to sleep,
Souls tossed in life's impenetrable deep:
Give me love's wisdom, that her soul divine,
May mingle all its loveliness with mine:
Then fill me with the music I create,

That I may find the depths of her sweet soul,
And hide me there, before it be too late.

It is unclear whether she does remain at Copeland for a further three years, but she is certainly still in England in 1924 because she is listed among the mourners at the funeral in London of her cousin, Kathleen Easmon Simango, the daughter of Mrs. Annette Easmon and sister of Charles Easmon.[5]

---OOOIIIOOO---

Kathleen, a fully-ledged Associate of the Royal College of Arts, had been living in Freetown with her mother when Gladys went away to school. She and her 'Auntie Addie' had felt concerned about the situation regarding the education of girls in Freetown. Mrs. Casely-Hayford writes in her memoirs,

> 'On the whole, apart from their rather sparse book knowledge, there was nothing to occupy their time, or to fit them for the battles of life. They received absolutely no practical training whatsoever. We felt that we must do something to better their condition, so we formed a committee of sympathetic Africans to foster a project of a visit to America. We wanted to investigate what was being done for the Afro-Americans to give them through vocational education, opportunities of standing on their own feet.' [6]

In 1920, with Gladys in Europe, the two women traveled to the United States where they also hoped to raise funds to start a vocational school for girls in Freetown. They spent two years visiting and giving lectures in various American cities, including New York, and it was there, at Columbia University, that they encountered an African graduate student called Columbus

Kambo Simango. He was from Portuguese East Africa, now Mozambique.

The young man promptly fell in love with the beautiful and talented Kathleen and she with him. After a brief courtship, they were married in Wilton, Connecticut in 1922. They sailed for Europe some months later and spent most of the next two years in Portugal, partly so that Kathleen could learn Portuguese before going to live in Simango's country. Unfortunately, that was not to be. Kathleen suffered an attack of appendicitis and, perhaps because of a delay caused by moving her from Lisbon to London for further treatment, succumbed to peritonitis at the Charing Cross Hospital on July 27, 1924.

From Mrs. Casely-Hayford's memoirs we learn that some time after Kathleen's funeral, Gladys returns to West Africa, though not to Freetown as her mother must have expected. She goes instead to the Gold Coast and, interestingly, works in the very field her headmistress at the Annie Walsh Memorial School thought would best suit her linguistic skills. She becomes a journalist for a weekly newspaper – the *Gold Coast Leader* – which her father co-founded in 1903 and has continued to publish from premises on Beulah Road, Cape Coast.

At least ten of the poems in Gladys's tattered collection are typed on letterheads of the *Gold Coast Leader*, and some, if not all, were probably published in that newspaper. One of these poems, entitled *Rejoice,* could be considered racist today, but taken in the context of the time when notions of the inferiority of black people were used to justify racial segregation and colonialism, it is merely a response to such attitudes. It heralds the empowering slogan, 'black is beautiful', which became current among African Americans in the 1960s:

Rejoice and shout with laughter
Throw all your burdens down,
If God has been so gracious

As to make you black or brown.

For you are a great nation,
A people of great birth
For where would spring the flowers
If God took away the earth?
Rejoice and shout with laughter
Throw all your burdens down.
Yours is a glorious heritage
If you are black or brown.

Gladys finally returns to Freetown early in 1926, summoned home by her mother who urgently needs assistance with the school she founded after her trip to America. Gladys, however, seems to have made several visits to the Gold Coast after that as she continues to be associated with the *Gold Coast Leader* until 1928. She reports on the proceedings of the 2nd Achimota Conference of the Congress of British West Africa in the issue of July 14, 1927, writes book reviews in the issues of August 20, 1927 and September 19, 1928, and publishes a poem dedicated to the late Dr. Aggrey in the issue of October 21, 1928.[7] Since it is one of those originally typed on the letterhead of the Gold Coast Leader, I have assumed that it is this poem:

To the Late Dr. Aggrey [8]

Can you let a fiery comet flash across our nation's night
And forget its brilliant passage when it vanishes from sight?

Can you hear the voice of patriotism rush up to the skies
And remember it with silence, with hard hearts and tearless eyes?

Can you let his mighty project for our country's common
good

Go unchampioned, unprotected, stagnant and
misunderstood?

Can you let a noble sacrifice of spirit, power and brain
Become a thing forgotten, till the memory be slain?

Oh Africa, my Africa, take back your quickened soil,
And cradle it with tenderness for its unceasing toil;

And bury it with reverence that out of you should spring
A Negro of such brilliance, who did so great a thing.
But let his wondrous memory live in you until the birth
Of brotherhood twixt black and white shall triumph o'er the
earth.

---OOOIIIOOO---

Mrs. Casely-Hayford, now lived on the first floor of 'Gloucester
House', a family property opposite the general post office on the
street of the same name. She established The Girls' Vocational
School on the ground floor in 1923, but since then, it had
struggled to survive. The forty girls who enrolled as foundation
pupils were all far too young to need vocational training, which
meant that she immediately had to scale down her ambitious
curriculum. That same year, she recruited as her assistant, Mrs.
Maisie Ejesa Osora, an English woman married to a Creole. Mrs.
Osora's employment immediately raised the enrollment of the
school to eighty pupils; but it soon became clear to Mrs. Casely-
Hayford that the disadvantages of having her on the staff far
outweighed the benefits. The main difficulty seems to have been
that while both women were united in their passion for educating

African girls, their personalities were deeply incompatible, both from all accounts being domineering individuals. However, in her memoirs Mrs. Casely-Hayford adds another dimension to the trouble between them:

> 'I might have known that as a white woman, even though she was married to a black man, she would never condescend to work under me.' [9]

After nine months, Mrs. Osora abruptly resigned and took most of the pupils with her to start 'The Osora Girls School'. Mrs. Casely-Hayford's health broke down under the strain of being abandoned in this ruthless fashion. In fact, she became so ill that the school's Management Committee had to grant her a long sick leave, hence the urgent call for Gladys's assistance.

Chapter Three

'Miss Gladys'

GLADYS must have been relieved to know that she did not have to take charge of the school. That duty had been assigned to a Mrs. Fred Miller, another former teacher at the Annie Walsh Memorial School. Still, her first teaching experience seems to have proved so stressful that, within a few months, she returns to the Gold Coast to recover from the strain.

Her mother received the news of her departure while on a second fund-raising trip to America. Since she was already at loggerheads with her Management Committee, this could only have added to her distress. In the end, the Management Committee closed down the school and resigned en masse; but, having regained her confidence by 1927, Mrs. Casely-Hayford reopened it. On this second attempt, she set up a three-man Advisory Board which she found much more helpful than the previous committee.

Gladys returns to Freetown. Through Mrs. Casely-Hayford's contacts in America, the school also gained the professional services of a young teacher called Elizabeth Torrey. Always referred to as 'Beth', Elizabeth Torrey was white and, astonishingly, from Georgia, one of the states in the Deep South of the United States where racial segregation was in those days institutional. Despite her background, Beth Torrey seems not to have had a single racist bone in her body. She lived with the Casely-Hayfords, shared a room with Gladys, and the two young women became close friends, sometimes lying awake at night to talk.

Apparently, Gladys often confided in Beth, saying she felt she could do so because she knew Beth's affection was genuine.[1] The following couplet is an indication of just how much she came to appreciate her new friend in the sixteen months that Beth spent in Freetown:

To Beth

She came to us between the storms and hushed torrential showers.
She brought her laughter with her, and filled our home with flowers.

In the course of her second trip to America, Mrs. Casely-Hayford had shown some of Gladys's poems to a friend who was so impressed that she sent them to the editor of the *Atlantic Monthly*, a well respected magazine.[2] The three shown below were selected for publication under a pen-name. This might have been suggested by the editors who may have wanted to romanticise Gladys, somewhat. She chose the name, 'Aquah Laluah', and was introduced to the readers as 'the grand-daughter of a native king', which was quite untrue since her maternal grandfather, William Smith Jr., had been a civil servant, and her paternal grandfather, a minister of religion.

Nativity [3]

Within a native hut, ere stirred the dawn,
Unto the Pure one was an infant born;
Wrapped in blue lappah that His mother dyed,
Laid on His father's home-tanned deerskin hide,
The Babe still slept, by all things glorified.
Spirits of black bards burst their bonds and sang
"Peace upon earth" until the heavens rang.
All the black babies who from earth had fled
Peeped through the clouds – then gathered round His head.

Telling of things a baby needs to do,
When first he opens his eyes on wonders new;
Telling Him that to sleep was sweetest rest,
All comfort came from His black mother's breast.
Their gift was Love, caught from the springing sod,
Whilst tears and laughter were the gifts of God.
Then all the Wise Men of the past stood forth,
Filling the air East, West, and South and North;'
And told him of the joy that wisdom brings
To mortals in their earthly wanderings.
The children of the past shook down each bough,
Wreathed frangipani blossoms for His brow;
They put pink lilies in His mother's hand,
And heaped for both the first fruits of the land.
His father cut some palm fronds, that the air
Be coaxed to zephyrs while He rested there.
Birds trilled their hallelujahs; all the dew
Trembled with laughter, till the Babe laughed too.
All the black women brought their love so wise,
And kissed their motherhood into His mother's eyes.

The Serving Girl

The calabash wherein she served my food
Was as smooth and polished as sandalwood;
Fish as white as foam from the sea,
Peppered, and golden fried for me.
She brought palm wine, that carelessly slips
From the sleeping palm tree's honeyed lips.
But who can guess, or even surmise,
Of the countless things she served with her eyes.

The Souls of Black and White [4]

The souls of black and white were made by the self-same
God of the self-same shade;

God made both pure, and He left one white, God laughed
o'er the other, and wrapped it in night.

Said he, "I've a flower, and none can unfold it, I've a breath
of great mystery, nothing can hold it."

Spirit so illusive the wind cannot sway it, a force of such
might even death cannot slay it."

But so that He might conceal its glow, He wrapped it in
darkness, that men might not know.

Oh, the wonderful souls of both black and white, were made
by one God, of one sod, on one night.

A few years later, three more of Gladys's poems appeared in
another American periodical called *Opportunity, a Journal of Negro
Life,*[5] these also probably submitted for publication by her
mother. A favourite of mine, shown below, is not among the
poems in Gladys's collection and therefore new to me:

The Palm Wine Seller

Akosua selling palm wine,
In the broiling heat;
Akosua selling palm wine
Down our street.

Frothing calabashes
Filled to the brim,
Boatmen quaffing palm wine
In toil's interim.

Tossing off their palm wine,
Boatmen deem her fair.
Through the haze of palm wine,
Note her jet black hair,

Roundness of her bosom,
Brilliance of her eyes,
Lips that form a Cupid's bow
Whereon love's dew lies.
Velvet gleam of shoulder,
Arch of bare black feet;
Soft caressing hands,
These her charms complete.

Thus illusioned boatmen
Dwell on 'Kosua's charms,
Blind to fallen bosom,
Knotted thin black arms.

Lips creased in by wrinkles,
Eyes dimmed with the years,
Feet whose arch was altered
Treading vales of tears.

Hair whose roots life's madness
Knotted and turned wild.
On her heart a load of care;
On her back a child.

Akosua selling palm wine
In the broiling heat.
Akosua selling palm wine
Down our street.

As a result of the publication of her poems in the *Atlantic Monthly*, Gladys was offered a place at the prestigious Radcliffe College for women in Massachusetts, but for some unexplained reason, and to the intense disappointment of her mother, she refused it. Mrs. Casely-Hayford must have been glad to have her at her school, however, for Gladys now threw herself into her work as a teacher. She composed not only the School Song, shown below, but one for the Brownies as well. She also wrote a song for African schoolgirls in general which I have included in Annex Two.

The School Song

The Girls Vocational School, may its spirit live for aye,
So cheer it, girls, with a mighty cheer and a hip, hip, hip,
hooray girls,
And a hip hip hip hooray.

Chorus: With a hip and a hip and a hip hip hip hooray!

We stand for truth and might and courage to meet each blow,
To form a part of Africa's heart that all the world may know
girls,
That all the world may know.

Chorus:

We stand for union and peace till joy and love
That our sons may share our faith and prayer, and scatter
sunshine round,
And scatter sunshine round.

Chorus:

We work with body and brain that intellect may
Give life the best and return the best and gain content and
peace,
And gain content and peace.

Chorus:

African Brownie Song

We are Brownies living in the land of Africa
We'll always try to lend a hand, to Africa.
Loyalty to God and the King, lend a hand we always sing
To Africa

We shall grow up brave and true for Africa,
Find some noble work to do, for Africa.
Loyalty to God and the King, lend a hand we always sing
To Africa.

Bless all Brownies in the world, where'ere they be.
Link us with the chains of love o'er land and sea.
Loyalty to God and King, lend a hand we always sing
To Africa.

Mrs. Casely-Hayford had clearly been influenced by her husband's staunch patriotism during the years of their marriage and, despite her generally European outlook, liked to wear African styles of dress when she felt that the occasion warranted it; she had done so whenever she had to make important speeches during her travels in America and also when the Prince of Wales visited Freetown in 1925. However, it is quite possible that it was Gladys, much more recently with J.E. Casely Hayford, who suggested the institution of 'Africa Day' at the school. Held every quarter, the intention of 'Africa Day' was to infuse the hearts and minds of the pupils with a spirit of love and loyalty towards their homeland and its people. [6] On 'Africa Day', all the pupils and staff, even Beth Torrey, came to school dressed in some form of African attire. Studies for the day were centred around Africa, its peoples past and present, its natural resources, its history, its customs, its folk tales and its arts and crafts. The programme for the day always included African songs, the performance of African dances, and African girls' games – one of which was probably the highly energetic *Akra* with its rhythmic handclapping and foot play.

My late mother, whose maiden name was Olivette Stuart, attended the Girls' Vocational School from 1928-1933 and often entertained us with stories about the time she spent there, about Mrs. Casely-Hayford's little ways, and about 'Miss Gladys', as she called her. The following poem, entitled *To My Little Friends*, suggests that the four Stuart sisters at the school, were among Gladys's favourite pupils:

There's Mary, she's the eldest,
Sometimes she's very nice.
There's Lettie, she's the primmest,
Most clever and precise.
Four year-old chubby Melvine,
She's a laughing hoyden yet,

Then twixt these two a shy one,
Little Lady Olivette.

Then here's to serious Mary,
May she grow a woman true,
And Lettie of the tidy mind,
We hope great things from you.
You, Melvine, chubby darling,
You'll grow big-hearted yet,
But yours will be an old world charm,
Sweet, timid Olivette.

Since I had no idea at the time that I would one day be
attempting to write a biography of Gladys, I did not realise how
fortunate I was to have those first-hand accounts of what she was
like as a teacher. From my mother's accounts, Gladys was full of
energy and fun, and composed songs to help the children
remember their lessons. My mother recalled some of them only
imperfectly, so I was absolutely delighted to discover one of her
favourites – *The Palm Tree* – among several poems inserted in
between Gladys's poetic retellings of West African folk tales.
With its notes, glossaries and questions, this book was apparently
one of her teaching tools:

The Palm Tree

What comes out of the palm tree,
the palm tree, the palm tree;
What comes out of the palm tree?
Why everything that's good.

Big umbrella,
When rains pour,
Keeps you dry

From door to door.

Makes a blye*
that will do,
To carry hens
Or keep fufu.**

Thatch for roofs,
Twisted thread,
Makes the yeast,
For your bread.

Fans and mats,
Candles, soap,
Palmoil, wine,
Hats and rope.

Cabbage for food,
Brooms to sweep,
Nuts to crack,
Rings to keep.

Don't you love the palm tree,
the palm tree, the palm tree,
Don't you love the palm tree,
that God has made for you?

Yes we love the palm tree,
the palm tree, the palm tree,
Yes we love the palm tree,
we do, we do, we do.

* *a basket*
** *a starchy food made from processed, slightly fermented cassava*

According to Gladys's notes, another of these poems was meant to accompany hygiene lessons:

Anatomy (The Body)

Children this is knowledge
That every child should know;
Just what God put inside us
To make us children grow.
Lungs to breath, heart to beat,
Liver to digest our meat;
Stomach to hold all our food,
Brains to learn just what we should.
The long spine from which nerves grow,
Like branches of a tree you know,
Through the body twist and thread
From tips of toes to crown of head.
Such bones God shaped within us all,
Wedged, curved and crooked, great and small.
The spine is made of bones like rings;
The shoulder blades are flat, like wings.

Then with kind purpose for our ease,
God wrapped firm muscles over these.
To give life to his work of art
He sent blood pumping through the heart.

It was interesting to learn from Archie Casely-Hayford's daughter, Desiree Sheldrake, that Gladys home-tutored her for a while in Accra using the same method of integrating poetry and other art forms with whatever subject she was teaching.

Since her main responsibility at the school was African folklore, it must have been during her years at the Girls'

Vocational School that Gladys started collecting West African folk tales. She retold them not only as narratives, but also as musical plays which featured prominently on 'Africa Days'. One of the most memorable of these musical plays, as far as my mother was concerned, was *The Magic Calabash*. Even well into her sixties, she remembered the story well, and being quite an actress, sometimes entertained young members of the family with her own version of it, playing the various parts and singing what she remembered of Gladys's songs. The entire story as told by Gladys has been included as Annex One at the end of this book. I inserted song lyrics at the most appropriate points in the story, but sadly, their tunes now live only in the unreliable memories of those who heard them.

Gladys also began to promote West African folk tales in the wider Freetown community. *The Sierra Leone Weekly News* of April 1929 [7] reports that she was the speaker at the Annual meeting of the Princess Christian Mission Hospital where she used the occasion to perform a retelling of a 'Nancie'(Ananse)* story.

'Miss Gladys' must have been an enormous asset to the Girls' Vocational School, even as she began to make a name for herself in the community, so this should have been a happy time for Mrs. Casely-Hayford. Gladys had, however, also begun to cause her such anxiety that their relationship entered a place of disharmony from which it never fully emerged.

*West African folk tale in which the clever hero is often a spider with human characteristics.

Chapter Four

A very difficult girl[1]

THIS is a good point at which to introduce Miss Anna Melissa Graves, a white American, former social worker and teacher, who, in seeking to prove the essential oneness of all humankind, became a world traveler and writer. Her travels eventually brought her to West Africa where she spent a week in Freetown with Mrs. Casely-Hayford early in 1931. The outcome of that short visit was a lively correspondence with both mother and daughter which lasted more than a decade. Anna Graves included their letters to her in the book she published after her travels in West Africa and they are the source of most of the available information about Gladys's life from about 1929 till 1942.

As the narrative unfolds, readers unfamiliar with Dr. Cromwell's biography of Mrs. Casely-Hayford might be surprised, perhaps even dismayed, to think that she and Gladys allowed Anna Graves to publish their correspondence, some of which is of a highly personal and sensitive nature. Indeed, Anna Graves herself writes in her final note on the letters that she hesitated over publishing them, wondering whether it was,

> 'better to think of the indiscretion, perhaps the real wounding, which the making public of the letters might involve, or to think of giving the world such wonderful proofs of our common humanity.[2]

Obviously, her desire to provide 'such wonderful proofs of our common humanity', overcame her scruples. It is not at all clear that Mrs. Casely-Hayford, well over seventy years old by the time Anna Graves came to publish the letters, knew exactly what her friend planned to do with them, as she claimed, or that Mrs. Casely-Hayford remembered in detail all that the correspondence contained. And even if she gave approval for their publication, there is no mention of Gladys's permission being sought before some of the most private and painful episodes in her life were revealed. However, everyone concerned passed on a long time ago and, as a result of Dr. Cromwell's biographical work, both the contents of the letters and Anna Graves's copious notes are now very much in the public domain. I, therefore, felt little hesitation in using the material myself, especially since Gladys's son, who happens to be my husband, had no objection to my doing so. Besides, Anna Graves played such a crucial role in Gladys's life that anyone trying to piece together the more obscure details of it can only be grateful for this wealth of information coming to light.

---OOOIIIOOO---

Mrs. Casely-Hayford realised quite early that although her daughter possessed innate wisdom and common sense, she was not a person one could describe as down-to-earth; 'harum-scarum' was the way Gladys described herself in one of her letters to Anna Graves. [3] However, until she entered her twenties, her mother seems to have adored her and tended to spoil her, especially because she had that slight disability. 'Gladys is a wonderful child, with an ethereal development of an exceedingly "high" order,' Mrs. Casely-Hayford enthuses in a letter to her husband written on August 9, 1921, when Gladys was seventeen. [4]

There were, in my opinion, two reasons why her attitude towards Gladys had changed by 1931 when Anna Graves came on the scene. First of all, being unusually independent-minded for a woman of her time, Mrs. Casely-Hayford wanted her daughter to make something of herself and become financially self-sufficient. Secondly, and this reason might have been the more important of the two, now sixty-three, she was staring old age in the face. Although they had never divorced, she received only a small allowance from her husband as part of their Separation Agreement, and any financial benefit gained from the school was far too little to inspire confidence that her old age could be made secure from that source. In any case, she knew she could not run the school forever; so even more worrying for her must have been the fact that Gladys, on whom she felt she would have to depend, was showing no inclination to take over as headmistress. Besides, even if Gladys had been interested in running the school, she still lacked any formal qualifications to do so. Remembering her niece, Kathleen Easmon, who had become an Associate of the Royal College of Arts, must have made Mrs. Casely-Hayford even more dissatisfied with that situation.

She never stopped accusing her husband of being responsible for her own daughter's lack of a college diploma, and may even have done so hurtfully in front of Gladys, who, according to Anna Graves, was devoted to her father. Complaining to Anna Graves about his neglect of Gladys, she wrote to say,

' The real person to blame in the whole business is her father. He never gave her a chance, and he could easily have done so, for he was a flourishing barrister…' [5]

In her growing anxiety about the future, Mrs. Casely-Hayford must have decided that for both their sakes, she needed to take Gladys more firmly in hand and make her not only use her literary talents for financial gain, but also to seize any opportunity to complete her education so she could eventually take over the school. Gladys must have exasperated her by cooperating in this scheme in a half-hearted manner, especially when it came to working on her writing. According to Anna Graves, Mrs. Casely-Hayford was, 'sure that it was just "pure cussedness" when she[Gladys] could not give birth to stories and poems as a rabbit produces or even as a tapster turns a spigot and draws beer or ale when called on'.[6]

Gladys was fully aware that she was no match for her mother when it came to a battle of wills so, according to both Beth Torrey and Charles Easmon in letters to Anna Graves, [7] the way she rebelled against her mother's demands was to exaggerate the pain in her disabled leg. Thus had the seeds of an unhealthy relationship been sown.

It was interesting to note that only two of the poems in Gladys's collection even mention her father. The first, *At the Dance* begins 'Find me some partners, Daddy, for I want to tread the wind…' and is not actually about him. The second one, which is untitled and I have seen only in her mother's *Profile of Gladys*, goes:

With Pa, I feel so lonesome,
'cause Mammy she ain't there.
With Ma, I feel like crying,
'cause of Daddy's empty chair.
Then when I start a-straining
at the leash to go away,
Ma wants a savoury omelette
– so I cook it and I stay.
Pa respects a person's feelings
an' he up and says to me
That as an individual,
I had certain rights, you see,
And he'd not encroach upon them;
Thus we struck a friendship true,
That will go on enduring

so long as skies are blue.
And when he says quite casual,
'Would you like some ginger beer?'
I just unpack my box again and say,
'Yes, Daddy, dear!'

Although written in a humorous pseudo-American style, I find this poem most revealing. In the lines beginning, 'Pa respects a person's feelings' up to 'Thus we struck a friendship true...' Gladys seems to be comparing her mother's attitude towards her unfavourably with her father's. Mr. Casely-Hayford perhaps recognised and accepted her free-spirited, artistic temperament and was prepared to let her dance to her own music, so to speak, probably expecting that she would be taken care of either by some future husband, or by himself.

Anna Graves mentions in her notes that when they first met, one reason for Mrs. Casely-Hayford's growing anxiety over Gladys was her daughter's love affairs. [8] Judging from the number of poems and songs Gladys wrote on the subject, love in all its forms was for her the very essence of living; she was also highly susceptible to the idea of being swept away by passion, as suggested in this poem:

Love Me

Love me, but whilst thou'rt loving, whisper not, "I love thee,"
or "How wonderful thou art!"
Drop thy warm kisses softly on my mouth, and let

Love me, but whilst thou'rt loving, let the night wrap its great
mantle o'er us from veiled skies;
Let the light be the fire flames leaping up in silent ardour
In thy dark brown eyes.

Love me, but whilst thou'rt loving, take me out of this great
world in silent ecstasy
Wing through love's aeons of space, and time, and place,
touching the borders of eternity.
Love me with tears, but love me silently.

However, from what I have been able to discover, Gladys
had only three suitors worth mentioning when she was in her
twenties. One of them was the Sierra Leonean composer and
scholar of indigenous African music, Nicholas Ballanta. An
informant close to the family told me that the relationship was
scuppered by Mrs. Casely-Hayford, though she had no idea why.
However, Charles Easmon informed Anna Graves in a letter that
it was Nicholas Ballanta himself who broke off the relationship
with Gladys.[9] Indeed, one wonders why Mrs. Casely-Hayford
would have rejected such a worthy suitor, especially one who
shared Gladys's passion for music. And besides, Nicholas
Ballanta was someone she herself had helped go to America to
research the tonal links between indigenous African and black
American music.[10]

It is likely that she simply did not want Gladys contemplating
marriage before she had acquired the all-important diploma
which would qualify her eventually to take over the school.
Another more intriguing possibility comes to mind, however: that
Mrs. Casely-Hayford who, according to one of Dr. Cromwell's
informants, had expressed the view that only the upper classes
should mingle, did not think that a 'village boy', no matter how
well educated and brilliant, was a fitting husband for any daughter
of hers.[11] If that were indeed her reason for putting a stop to
Nicholas Ballanta's courtship, the irony of it will be revealed as
Gladys's story unfolds. In any case, if Mrs. Casely-Hayford did
kill the romance, she must have done so with subtlety and
discretion because it is hard to imagine that her nephew, with
whom she appears to have been close, would not have known

about her part in it. On the other hand, Charles Easmon might have known about his aunt's part in ending the love affair, but thought Anna Graves had pried into their family's private affairs quite enough, and so gave her an answer meant to forestall further questions on the matter.

Another suitor, of whom there is evidence, was a mysterious 'Humphrey' who seems to have been an Afro-Caribbean, brought up in England but who, for some reason, later migrated to Sierra Leone. One of Beth Torrey's letters to Anna Graves provides a little more information about Humphrey:

> '...he was musical and had sung 'Old Man River' on the London stage before the great [Paul] Robeson came to oust him out of the place. I have been many places (no not many – a few) and met many coloured people, but he stands right up near the top of the list for me. Of course, he was to a large extent English as well as being Negro...' [12]

From the available evidence, Gladys's relationship with him could hardly have been described as a love affair. Anna Graves mentions in her notes that Beth Torrey, who was close to both parties, informed her that Humphrey was desperately in love with Gladys, but when he realised that his pursuit of her was hopeless, gave it up and later married an uneducated Liberian woman.[13] Incidentally, so did Ballanta, according to my informant. Beth thought Humphrey took that step because he was desperate and did not care what happened to him when Gladys refused to marry him. Gladys, according to Beth,

> 'did not quite appreciate Humphrey and played with him too much'. [14]

In her own correspondence, Mrs. Casely-Hayford told Anna Graves that she knew nothing whatsoever about Gladys's love for

Humphrey and would have been only too pleased to welcome him as a son-in-law; that he never approached her to ask for Gladys's hand, and that she had had no idea their relationship was more than 'the ordinary boy and girl friendship.'[15]

Mrs. Casely-Hayford's recollection of the episode is consistent with Beth Torrey's that Gladys had only flirted with Humphrey.

I found all this confusing at first because Anna Graves mentions in her notes that Gladys herself accused her mother of preventing her marriage to Humphrey. The reason for my confusion became clear as I read more of Anna Graves's notes. She obviously thought Humphrey and Nicholas Ballanta were one and the same person, even referring to 'Humphrey Ballata'(sic) at one point.[16] Since she had only heard about these relationships from other people, she must have mixed up the two men in her mind, and seems to have confused them further with Gladys's third suitor. It is about third suitor that Mrs. Casely-Hayford expressed anxiety. More about that relationship will be revealed in due course.

---OOOIIIOOO---

Given what Mrs. Casely-Hayford herself referred to as her 'Napoleonic spirit of domination',[17] her financial worries about the future, and her high expectations of Gladys, it is easy to imagine that by 1928 she was putting her daughter under a good deal of pressure to do something about acquiring a college diploma and getting more of her poems published. It must have been a time of arguments, recriminations and tears for Gladys later complained to Anna Graves, perhaps unfairly, that her mother saw her only as her successor at the school or as the author of 'Nativity', and that she sometimes wished she had never written the poem.[18] However, though she might often have felt angry and rebellious, judging from the number of poems she wrote about Mrs. Casely-Hayford, there is no doubt that Gladys both admired and loved her mother. Take this one, for example;

Jealous

Her sweet smile is angelic
Because she's nearer heaven,
Than I who am but twenty-two,
Whilst Mother's fifty-seven.

I'm like some unplucked fruit,
Mother is warm and mellow,
Men term her charmingly discreet,
But dub me 'a good fellow'.

She's like a cameo,
Set in an old world frame,
They call her 'dear Adesha'
But 'Bobby' is my name.

My black hair is unruly,
Her hair is silken white,
Her eyes are pools of wisdom,
Whilst mine are starry night.

I'm vigorous, strong and vital;
Langorous, graceful, free,
Are Mother's quiet movements,
Like old world courtesy.

I know I'm losing grace,
But where's the room for heaven,
With mothers floating round the place,
Glorious at fifty-seven?

It could only have been in response to her mother's persistent fault-finding that Gladys wrote these moving lines:

To My Mother

I cannot give you perfect happiness, or luxury or wealth,
opulent ease,
For God provides the first and fate the last; but I can give
you these:
The smile of welcome, the fresh bloom of youth, the happy
fount of laughter and the shield
Of young protectiveness and two strong arms to fold you in
when wearied; strength to wield
My small affairs unto their highest light, to stand between you
and life's constant fight.
Not officiously, but with a care that's bred of helpless swift
anxiety and tears
For what I cannot do, and for your years.
These I can give you, and creative art
From the full flowing fountain of my heart.

As Mrs. Casely-Hayford tells it in her profile, Gladys,

'…casually posted some specimens of her work to Columbia University and immediately received an invitation to migrate there without delay.'[19]

Bearing in mind that Gladys had refused an offer to enter Radcliffe College just a couple of years earlier, one has a strong suspicion that, as previously happened, it was her mother who pressed her to send samples of her poetry to Columbia, or even did so on her behalf. When the poems received such an enthusiastic response, she put pressure on Gladys to take up the offer of a place. Indeed, before she came to write the *Profile of Gladys*, Mrs. Casely-Hayford had admitted to Anna Graves that Gladys never wanted to go to Columbia, but that she wanted her to go because she had been accepted as a student, in spite of the deficiencies in her formal education.[20]

Before this, Gladys, probably with an idea of escaping from her mother's constant nagging, had begun to save all the money she could spare. This time she agreed to go to America and Columbia University but, in the light of future developments, it is abundantly clear that she was never committed to the project.

Chapter Five

Seeking freedom

AS if she has a premonition that this is going to be a momentous year, Gladys begins 1929 by writing this poem:

The New Year

Another year has dawned.
Who knows what sorrow,
What measure of new hope for the new morrow,
What gladness lies still folded in its days,
What brightness will emblazon its new maze,
What glory on life's age-old routine shine,
What struggle may ignite from sparks divine.
How many souls will draw the babe's first breath.
How many more will pass the gates of death?
Another year has dawned, and with its dawning
Of sunshine, birds and flowers, and hazy morning,
Lord in Thy mercy unto us appear,
With loving tenderness be very near
To guide us safely through another year.

She has purchased a typewriter from her savings which now amount to eighty pounds sterling. Her mother gives her an additional forty pounds and, thus equipped, before the summer of 1929 she leaves Freetown for America, traveling through England. I have found no evidence that she visited her father before leaving Africa, which seemed rather odd, until I realised that she probably visited him during the latter half of 1928 when she contributed book reviews and a poem to *The Gold Coast*

Leader. In any case, every available pound must have been earmarked for the Columbia project.

On her arrival in London, Gladys goes to the American Embassy only to discover that she will need another thirty pounds in order to obtain a visa for the States. While waiting for her mother to send her the additional funds, she tries various temporary jobs and finally joins a troupe of African street entertainers. In spite of her physical impairment, Gladys persuades the leader of the troupe – an Egyptian called Hassen – to hire her as a dancer. That Christmas, the entertainers move to Berlin and, having decided to postpone going to America, Gladys goes with them.

She spends the next three months dancing for a living and, among other ventures to boost her meagre earnings, makes baskets for sale and writes songs which were presumably performed. She later tells Anna Graves that she worked at every job she could find and worked overtime, not only to spare her mother the financial burden of having to support her in Germany, but also to pacify her by saving money to go to Columbia.[2] She says that trying to get to Columbia reduced her 'to nights of pain and days of tears.' Her writing also suffers as a result of the many demands on her time and energy, not to mention her domestic arrangements which are hardly conducive to creative pursuits, since she has to share a room with three other female members of the troupe. Nevertheless, she continues to work in a desultory way on the words and music of a song entitled 'God's overalls' (missing from her collection), on a detective novel set in Freetown, and another book about the colour problem, entitled 'Shadowed Livery.' None of these manuscripts have been traced.

It is not at all surprising to learn that Gladys eventually becomes ill enough to be admitted to a hospital in Berlin, her treatment covered by a small health insurance. It must have been there that she wrote, "Noelendorf Klinik" on April 2, 1930.

Down the muted corridor the white clad Sister goes
To smooth the wrinkled pillow, and creases of pain unclose,
As deft and quick as the fingers of God, fashioning the heart
of a rose.
When the doctor, aided by science, closes the gates of pain,
A smile gleams through the patient's tears, like the sun
through April rain,
the poor wracked body is quietened, and sleep comes once
again.
Do not be discouraged, oh workers, never your calling regret;
Though the day may teem with worry, and the patients harass
and fret,
Some who are healed will always remember; God will never
forget.

Gladys did not specify the nature of this illness which
apparently lasted quite a while but, given the strain she had put
on her left hip and leg, her hectic lifestyle, and also the mention
of 'creases of pain' and the 'poor wracked body' in 'Noelendorf
Klinik', it was probably some debilitating and extremely painful
ailment such as sciatica. In one of her letters to Anna Graves, she
mentions a nerve twisted in her spine.[3] When the news of her
father's death on August 11, 1930 reaches her, she is, in her own
words, 'utterly devastated' for, as she tells Anna Graves, they
loved each other very dearly.

Despite all that hardship and suffering, however, Gladys does
not sound actually miserable in the letters from this period of her
life. She must have been relishing the freedom of being far away
from her mother and among people as free-spirited as herself, as
well as the adventure of being her own person while gaining a
great deal of interesting life experience. She seems to have lived
harmoniously with her room-mates, especially the one she

mentions by name called 'Amy', whom she describes as having a lovely singing voice.

Meanwhile, Gladys writes to tell Anna Graves that even while she was still in very low spirits following the death of her father, her mother kept insisting that she should go to Columbia:

> 'I did not feel equal to it...I was by this time scared of life itself. No, I must go to Columbia, Mother insisted. I dared not return home to days of teaching and sometimes lying on my back because of my foot, and getting nowhere, so in sheer desperation, I said I would go.' [4]

In the end, despite feeling certain that she will never survive the Columbia experience and praying that another way might open up at least to assure her mother of a home, in October 1930, Gladys writes home to say that one of her uncles visited her, sorted out the visa problems and she is now ready to travel whenever the necessary funds arrive from Freetown.

It took Mrs. Casely-Hayford some time to collect the required amount. She later told Anna Graves that she had 'to deprive herself of some of the bare necessities of life' to do so. As fate would have it, by the time the money reaches Gladys, she has received two proposals of marriage and ecstatically accepted one of them.

She had apparently fallen deeply in love with another member of the troupe—a young man from the Cameroons whom we know only by the nickname, 'Big Boy', because Anna Graves had forgotten his real name by the time she came to publish the letters. It might well have been on account of 'Big Boy' that Gladys went off to Germany with the troupe in the first place, and for him that she wrote this blissful song in October 1929:

My Boy

You may know captains or princes or kings,
And heroes or philosophers who're wise in many things.
Men who know earth's secrets
or guide the seaplane's wings,
But you don't know My Boy.

You may have seen Venice,
or heard Baghdad's street cries,
Or Cairo or India, or soft blue English skies.
But you've not seen
the beauty hidden deep in someone's eyes.
You haven't seen My Boy.

You may have heard music, the laughing saxophone,
The piano, the violin, the viol and trombone.
But I've heard laughter sweeter than any music known;
You haven't heard My Boy.

'Oh, he's wonderful! He's marvelous!
He brings me peace and joy.
Why do I love him? I don't know,
It's 'cause he's just…My Boy!'

Having accepted 'Big Boy's proposal of marriage, any thoughts of going to Columbia simply fly out of Gladys's mind and she announces her engagement to her mother. She later tells Anna Graves that her mother's response had been that she would give her consent if Gladys loved 'Big Boy';[5] but given the circumstances, that sounds rather like a wishful interpretation of Mrs. Casely-Hayford's answer on Gladys's part. To make matters even worse, Gladys now decides that, having found the ideal partner, she will leave the troupe with him and together they will put on a show of their own. She recklessly sinks all available funds into the production, including the money her mother has sent for the journey to America, and pours all her energy into the project. It is therefore easy to imagine her utter dismay when, despite their hard work, the revue is a flop. Chastened, she admits to Anna Graves that,

'I should have thought more, been more cautious and not spent all that… I have been foolish, I know. ' [6]

She gives as her reasons for embarking on such a risky venture her certainty that she would double her investment, and that she needed some completely absorbing project to help her face life again after her father's death. [7]

Gladys and 'Big Boy' now find themselves almost penniless at a time when jobs are scarce in Germany and especially so, one imagines, for black people. Mrs. Casely-Hayford has known about the revue and has, of course, denounced the scheme as 'idiotic'. She does not, however, learn about its disastrous consequences until, at the point of starvation and owing rent on her room, Gladys desperately cables her with another plea for financial help. Once again, she sends Gladys some money which she uses to settle her debts and buy nourishing food before, 'shaken and disappointed', as she later tells Anna Graves, she picks herself up and signs another contract with Hassen.

By this time, Mrs. Casely-Hayford must have been like a smouldering volcano, and her fury must have erupted when 'Big Boy', wrote formally to ask for Gladys's hand in marriage. She told Anna Graves,

'I do not want her to marry a man who lives by his wits. He has no trade, no steady employment of any kind and I cannot bear to think of her placing her life in his keeping. I suggested that he should go to a night school to learn mechanical engineering, when he might stand a chance of a steady government post in the Kameroons, but he has never replied.' [8]

Gladys later confides to Anna Graves, that 'Big Boy' found her mother's letter so insulting that he immediately broke off their engagement. Interestingly, Gladys seems to have thought that her mother's objection to him also had something to do with his colour – perhaps he was very dark-skinned as well as tall. Mrs. Casely-Hayford vigorously denied this, however, telling Anna Graves that Gladys was doing her a grave injustice if she thought she disapproved of the young man 'because of his background or colour.' [9]

Devastated by this turn of events, Gladys tells Anna Graves,

'I have not got over it, and shall never be the same girl. Something in me is dead now.' [10]

Such a dramatic expression of grief leads me to believe that she wrote the following mournful songs during that period of desperate financial hardship and emotional turmoil. The first one is dated February 11, 1931, which makes the timing right; and they both seem to reflect recent happenings in her life.

The Might Have Been

I cannot blame you for what is past.
Fate took a hand in it, joy did not last.
Misunderstanding held us in thrall,
Better for both had we ne'er met at all.

When I think of the joy that might have been,
Had the dream of our love come true,
When I think of the grey in the skies above,

That should have been glorious blue.

When I think of the waste of the best life holds,
And the empty receipt of the years,
When I think of the golden might have been,
It fills my eyes with tears.

The Down and Out Blues

I've got the down and out blues,
Nothing in my pockets and holes in both my
shoes.
Nothing in my inside, nothing on my head,
Ain't no roof to cover me, haven't got no bed.
I've got the down and out blues.

Ain't nobody's baby, ain't loved by no soul;
Ain't got no fine papa to hand me out the dole.
I ain't got no tears left; when I laugh I choke,
Life's a mess, I tell you, living ain't no joke.
I've got the down and out blues.

---OOOIIIOOO---

In spite of what she would describe as her daughter's 'callous, heartless, utterly selfish indifference'[11] to her welfare, Mrs. Casely-Hayford, did not give up her ambitions for Gladys. A strong believer in the power of prayer, her guiding principle was, 'When in doubt – Get down on your knees.'[12] The answer to what must have been months of constant supplication to the Almighty came in the person of Anna Graves. Their correspondence began in February 1931, right at the time when her relationship with Gladys was at its most turbulent. She soon drew Anna Graves into her confidence and when she learned that she was going to live in Geneva, pleaded with her to get in touch with Gladys and befriend her.

By the spring of 1931, Gladys and the troupe have moved on to Stockholm in Sweden, where they continue to earn a precarious living with their street entertainments.

An opportunity to promote the friendship came through one of those strange twists of fate – or by the hand of God, as Mrs. Casely-Hayford would no doubt have seen it. That June, an organisation called Save the Children International Union was holding a Conference on the African Child in Geneva. Mrs. Casely-Hayford had been chosen to represent the British West African colonies but had also been informed that, on account of the global economic recession, she would have to meet some of the costs of her attendance herself. Funds for that purpose had been raised by various women's groups in the British colonies along the west coast. The largest contribution had come not from the Freetown group, among many of whom Mrs. Casely-Hayford, though well respected, was not well liked, but from the Lagos Women's League. In the end, the money raised had proved insufficient to cover her trip to Geneva; but then she had a brainwave. With the approval of the Lagos Women's League, she asked Gladys to represent her, since travel from one European city to another would cost hardly anything.[13] She also hoped that going to Geneva would give Gladys's literary work much needed exposure and also remove her for good from the influence of her undesirable associates.

It should by now be clear to the reader that Mrs. Casely-Hayford regarded the twenty-seven-year-old Gladys as a child, and a wayward one at that. In many of her letters to Anna Graves she refers to her as, 'my little delicate erring daughter', 'the dear child', 'little Gladys' 'my little girl', 'the poor child', 'my poor little girl,' 'my precious little daughter,' and so on, while complaining bitterly about her behaviour. To be scrupulously fair, though, she also used the qualifier 'little' when referring to Beth Torrey and other young women, so it was perhaps a habit of hers. However, in the case of Gladys, it does suggest an attitude of always knowing best which is consistent with her character.

No matter how justified she felt it to be, that attitude was hardly likely to foster a harmonious relationship with a young woman who craved a life of her own and wanted to establish her own identity. To her mother, Gladys may have seemed an irresponsible underachiever, but Gladys considered herself an adult and as such, entitled to live her life the way she wanted to, even if she did need financial help from time to time. Calmly accepting that state of affairs would have been difficult for most parents. For someone with Mrs. Casely-Hayford's temperament and financial anxieties, it was impossible.

Beth Torrey makes the case for Gladys in a letter to Anna Graves:

'Gladys is quite old enough to begin making her own mistakes, even to the drastic one of marrying a 'bum'. [14]

Gladys herself puts it in a more measured, but no less emphatic way:

'I agree with you that she [her mother] is an extraordinary, a wonderful woman. I know that, and I admire her tremendously. But at the present stage of my development she would help me more by sinking her own personality into the background, and by letting me find my own and develop it in my own way, instead of trying to mould me: that is my only point of contention. Nothing else. In another two or three years, when I have got through this period, I shall be only too pleased to return home where I belong; but at present I want to be just let alone.' [15]

In another letter to Anna Graves, she makes this telling remark:

'I am so glad you seem to understand me. I do not want a friend who keeps telling me what to do. I need one who guides without seeming to; and who loves wisely without telling me every minute about it, and I think that is you.' [16]

As in the verse about her father which I have already mentioned, in this letter Gladys seems to be implying that such understanding does not exist between herself and her mother; and indeed, Mrs. Casely-Hayford acknowledges that. [17]

It is significant that when it did not concern Gladys, her attitude was much more tolerant; when Anna Graves told her about problems she was having with an adopted son, she replied, "Young people must buy their experience for themselves."[18] And she did have some insight into her attitude towards Gladys, attributing it to over-anxiety for her daughter's welfare which made her '… very short-sighted as to her point of view;' but in that same letter, she also laid bare her other major concern when she complained,

'Just imagine her leaving here 2 years ago for Columbia…and today she is still eking out a miserable existence, and I getting older and older with no one upon whom I can depend, but her.' [19]

---OOOIIIOOO---

As it turned out, the idea of letting Gladys represent her mother at the Geneva Conference was an excellent one. Having recovered a little from the loss of her father and the end of her engagement to 'Big Boy', Gladys readily agrees to go, telling Anna Graves that she is extremely interested in children.[20] She arrives in Geneva a few days early in order to become acquainted with both Anna Graves and the city before the conference begins, and she stays behind for about ten days afterwards. The break does her a world of good – so much so that on her return to Stockholm, she writes to tell Anna Graves that her friend, Amy, has started calling her 'Fatty'.

Gladys makes quite an impression at the conference, according to Anna Graves. She speaks several times in '...her most unusually charming speaking voice...' One short speech so wins over the delegates that some of them remark afterwards that her words have been the most sincere, yet tactful, spoken in all the meetings. Members of the various delegations seek her out – the Bahais who are interested in her African nursery folk songs and stories, as well as people interested in African music.[21] Mr. A.G. Fraser, principal of Achimota School in the Gold Coast, is so impressed that he offers her a teaching position as soon as she finishes her studies.[22]

Even as she makes her way back to Stockholm, Gladys continues to impress the people she meets. In her first letter to Anna Graves after the conference, she describes an incident on the ferry crossing to Scandinavia. She encountered 'a rather distinguished looking gentleman,' while wandering around in search of a cup of tea. He not only escorted her to the tea room, but asked whether he could sit beside her, to which she agreed so as not to appear ungracious. In the course of their conversation, the man asked what she thought of British rule, and Gladys, true offspring of J.E. Casely-Hayford, told him that there seemed not much to choose between any of the ruling powers; that Africans, like the Indians, would prefer no rule at all. The man persisted in saying that he thought British rule better than American, to which Gladys responded with a question: whether it was better to crush the individuality of a race or to hurt them physically. It turned out that the man was the British Consul in Sweden, and the next morning, to Gladys's astonishment, he called on her with the

Czechoslovakian Consul and another friend.[23] He must have brought them to meet this unexpectedly well informed and articulate young African woman.

Anna Graves herself grew so fond of Gladys that she confesses in her notes that from then onwards, her real sympathy was for her rather than for her mother who was always so completely sure of herself and the rightness of her opinions and actions. However, she did agree that Gladys was getting nowhere with the theatrical troupe and that, though she obviously had a great talent for writing, she would benefit from critical advice and more training and practice in the techniques of versification. After some reflection, she came to the conclusion that Gladys's educational needs would be better met at Ruskin College in Oxford, England [24] than at Columbia University. Besides, the expense of her going there would be considerably less. The principal of Ruskin College, a Mr. Barratt Brown, happened to be a good friend of hers, and when she told him about Gladys, he became interested enough to offer her a place at the College.[25]

Although, according to Anna Graves, Mrs. Casely-Hayford had once expressed the view that Africans stood a better chance of success in America than in Britain, she did not need much convincing that they should proceed with this new plan. Anna Graves now took over her role, though with considerably more tact, one imagines. As a result, Gladys agreed to go to Ruskin College.

Chapter Six

Unwilling surrender

AFTER reading through the prospectus Anna Graves has sent her, Gladys seems at first to be fairly enthusiastic about the prospect of going to study in England. She plans to start with the term beginning on September 28, 1931 which she says will coincide with the end of her contract with Hassen. On July 10, 1931 she writes to Anna Graves,

'I notice they require two letters in regard to the character of the applicant; I was wondering whether you would be kind enough to write one for me. I shall also get one from my employer – Hassen, and one from the Kuhs journalist friend of mine in Berlin. They require also a doctor's certificate of health; and as soon as I have found out what doctor to go to for an examination, I shall go. These seem to be the only difficulties in filling up the enclosed formula.

I think it would be far better for me to live out of College so as not to shift my home every two minutes, that is to say for every holiday. I do not think I shall be spending them out of Oxford, because I have nowhere especially to go, neither shall I be able to afford it. I am sure it will be possible to find two empty rooms somewhere and to furnish them myself. Another reason is that I do most of my work at night, and consequently I find it difficult to be punctual at breakfast. Rules state that rooms must be tidy by so and so, and silence at this and that time; these restrictions though necessary to the welfare of the community as a whole would get in the way of my work, as I hate to stop in the middle of a chapter for a meal, etc. In the long run I do not think it will cost so very mush more, if I furnish second hand. I really do long for a home in which I can potter about and make some things look African with my own curtains, etc. You do understand, don't you?'

Later in the letter she adds,

'I do not consider that there is time to wait for Mother's decision in this matter, I do not wish to lose the September term, and waiting for her replies in this case will mean missing it. Knowing that I have arrived at this decision with your help, will I am sure meet her warmest approval.' [1]

That initial enthusiasm, however, seems to have been all but extinguished by what must have been another hurtful letter from her mother – probably one containing more recriminations about all the money and time Gladys had wasted by joining the troupe of entertainers, as well as a stern warning against repeating such behaviour. Deeply wounded, Gladys writes to Anna Graves on July 14, 1931,

'Mother expects a quick return for the money spent on me. It is evident she finds financing the scheme a burden, to say nothing of my being 27 and having accomplished nothing. Under these circumstances I see no reason why I should be further indebted to her; since at the present moment I see no way of paying her back. She says I am no help to her; on the other hand, I am no hindrance. I can make my own way and keep myself my own way without any further (academic) degrees.

I am in a blue funk about starting at Ruskin, because Mother seems to think that all I have to do is to go in to College and write. Suppose she spends - say another £45 for my first term, I go to Ruskin, and nothing tangible happens – except contacts, and my novel still hangs fire. Mother will only blow me up some more for wasting her money.

So if I go to Ruskin I'm going to wait till I can pay my own way there. There must by no worry attached to it in regard to paying back cash. If I accept any more from Mother it will resolve itself into that.

I must prove my own worth as a writer first, get my novel out, finish 'God's overalls' and then put those things to the test. I can do that in a small room in Berlin, get the books I have o study second hand, and get some more of my work on the market and try to sell. After that, if I'm a dud it's my own fault. Perhaps I might yet be able to keep myself at Ruskin by short story writing. I don't know. I must see – must find out. If between that time and next June, for instance, I have achieved something – then Ruskin. If not – I'm not worth worrying about.

I prefer simple food, one room, my books and quiet for the present and no financial worry, to one term at Ruskin and a definite split with my mother at the end of it. [2]

An even more impassioned letter follows the next day, July 15, 1931. Apparently, Mrs. Casely-Hayford had written to Anna Graves again complaining about Gladys's attitude, absolutely rejecting any idea of her living off-campus, and giving as reasons Gladys's behaviour over going to Columbia. Anna Graves must have brought up the subject with Gladys and this is her reply:

'First and foremost: I had not thought that a room outside Oxford would cost so much, even two rooms. I am going by

German standards where things are cheap. I have been away from England. I listen to reason when things are pointed out to me. I am not wild, perhaps not as practical as I might be. I merely stated what I should like to do. I am, of course, willing to abide by your decision in things I know nothing about, as in the above case; and I'd promise, I think, anything you wanted, within reason, 'cause I like you.'

She goes on,

'How many people accomplish as much in two years, as I have with my handicaps? I am not a parasite, and never intend to be - never have been. At home I earned my keep and saved to get away. In Europe I made my money and lost it. I shall make it again; I have already started. I see nothing for it but to return as much of the money as I can, as soon as I can, and finish that. I am certainly not going to any Ruskin or to any other place if Mother feels that strain so much and is liable to blow up unless I do exactly what she wishes.

I don't want to go to Ruskin and later write to my mother, from sheer duty: "Enclosed herewith so and so, hope you will find it useful. Gladys."…I want to write, "Mother darling, I have had an awful year of it, but by George! this is the present from my FIRST Short Story in Nash's. You come first; just as soon as I have published ten more I'm coming right home to take you in my arms and comfort you, and look after you; because I shall be able to work at home now; I've got my connections, I'm a writer.'

You see I must have someone to love, and if I can't love Big Boy I must love Mother; and at the rate we are going there won't be any love left by the time we have finished – only obligations on both sides.'

She, however, ends on a humorous note:

'…I am going to post this.

And 'this' will make you think me very wild, I am afraid; but I am really quite harmless. I sound wilder that I really am.' [3]

It is obvious from Gladys's next letter to Anna Graves that their discussion about her conflict with her mother has continued, for in it she says,

'I don't agree with all your views, though. I like to handle my own money. If I promise to use a certain sum of money for a certain thing I do it, and if I say I'm going to Ruskin, I'll go; and I won't do anything else.'

One can well imagine Mrs. Casely-Hayford's sceptical snort had she heard Gladys make that assertion. Gladys continues,

'But I don't want any more money from home. To begin with I am not at all sure that there is any to have. Mother's letters are positive in one mail and negative in the next, besides being utterly inconsistent. One moment I'm a 'brave girl', the next I'm 'no use'; in one letter 'you are the only joy of my life' and in the next 'you are selfish and think only of yourself and are nothing but a burden and a worry. You neglect your duty to me.' Under the circumstances it is like walking on a wobbling plank, and I've had enough of it. Besides, Mother wishes to see financial results.'

Gladys goes on to tell Anna Graves how she intends to earn her living on her return to Germany from Sweden.

'In Winter there are usually films or plays that require coloured crowds. You can earn from 6 to 8, or even 10 marks a night, as long as the play runs. Films pay at the rate of 30 to 35 marks each time we work. Sitting as a model is paid at the rate of 1.25 or 3.00 or 4.00 marks for good private artists per hour. Lessons to Germans in English conversation at 1.50 the hour. These fill the winter months; in March, April and May the troupes start out again. All you do is join another troupe every summer and write every winter. It seems simple enough to me.' [4]

However, with Anna Graves acting as go-between and calmer of troubled waters, by the end of July, 1931, Gladys has made a kind of peace with her mother and the plan for her to go to Ruskin is back on track. However, since the financial problems have still not been resolved, it is beginning to look as if her going there might have to be postponed until December, 1931, or even January of 1932.

Mrs. Casely-Hayford kept hoping that she will receive a financial bequest mentioned in her late husband's will; but one year after his death, his estate had still not been wound up.[5] Gladys meanwhile, continues with her normal hectic life. She accompanies Amy and 'Big Boy' on the piano when they perform negro spirituals and jazz, for which they 'usually get a good clap at the end.' [6] She also continues to make baskets, experiments with making dolls representing different African characters, does her share of house work, and sells handicrafts at her stall. She tells Anna Graves that to earn money when her present contract ends, she is thinking of joining a Senegalese dance troupe which has recently arrived in Stockholm. [7]

Absolutely determined that nothing should prevent Gladys from going to Ruskin and making a success of herself at last, Mrs. Casely-Hayford continued to pile on the pressure. Gladys writes to tell Anna Graves,

'Mother's letters throw me into a sort of panic. I feel that I am not getting there – that she is always demanding something I can't do, either because I haven't the money to do it, or that mentally I am too tired to complete work begun, or that I can't do it in my present environment. It's: 'Have you done this?' or 'Are you going to do that?' 'What about that poem?' or 'this music?' [8]

Apparently, the conflict had now moved on to where her fees should be sent. Anna Graves, her hitherto trusted friend and confidante, told her that it would be a good thing if Mrs. Casely-Hayford paid the College direct for her board, lodging and tuition, adding that it would make her mother feel easier; that Mrs. Casely-Hayford would not be worrying, fearing the money was being spent unwisely, and that perhaps Gladys was not getting the kind of nourishment she should be having because she had decided a play meant more than dinner. To strengthen her case, Anna Graves added that Gladys would find it a great relief not to have to think about how to make ends meet. She, however, overplayed her hand. Ignoring the fact that Gladys was in her late twenties, she also tried to convince her that such an arrangement was no disgrace, since other parents usually sent cheques directly to colleges to meet their children's expenses. She insists in her notes that all this advice was so as to avoid letters from Mrs. Casely-Hayford to Gladys demanding to know how her money was being spent. Gladys, however, did not take it kindly and informed Anna Graves that she had suggested that arrangement to her mother herself.

Indeed, she had probably discussed the matter with her mother and, under pressure, simply resigned herself to falling in with Mrs. Casely-Hayford's wishes. However, having to give in on this issue must have rankled, especially since Anna Graves seemed to have joined her mother in thinking her too irresponsible to be trusted with money. Anna Graves annoyed and disappointed her further by a withering attack on her fiancé. [9]

Apparently. Gladys had written to tell her that, though she still planned to go to Ruskin, she and 'Big Boy' had become re-engaged, and she would therefore not be arriving in England until a month or so after College opened. Anna Graves remembers strongly criticizing 'Big Boy' in her reply for allowing a delay which might put Gladys in danger of losing her place at the college. Gladys's response is polite but frosty:

'You do blow me up, don't you? Please don't damn my future husband; I do not like that idea at all. Big Boy is not to blame for the delay. It is financial. He himself thinks it is best for me to go; but I must get to Ruskin with at least five pounds spending money in my pocket. By staying here another fortnight I get my fare paid back to Berlin, or another job for two months. I have a winter coat to get, and I have no warm underclothing either. All these things cost money; and what you can make shift with in a room by yourself you cannot wear in a College. I am not talking of luxuries – only necessities. My fare to London and thence to Oxford will cost a bit – even third (class). I must spend a night or two in London. I have to sort out an accumulation of clothes and things in Berlin – don't forget I have been there two years – and what I cannot use has to be sent home. That sorting will take a week at least. I cannot start out with what I have now, since Mother says I have to get myself there plus my wardrobe.

Sorry I have no time for more now. I am really beginning to be happy again now; all things seem to be working together for good.' [10]

Then in her very next letter, Gladys drops a bombshell:

'I am afraid what I have to communicate will upset you, rather. I am really sorry to grieve you; but absolute honesty is the best policy.   As I told you in my previous letter Big Boy and I are re-engaged; and we, with Amy and two other men have signed a contract for African singing and dancing. (P.S. I don't dance).

I have made a clean breast of it to Mr Barratt Brown: Mother does not approve of Big Boy, so that I can't very well go to Ruskin, can I? Besides it will entail an awful lot of sacrifice on her, which is not necessary. If I received this tuition, got more into debt and then married Big Boy, it would be, to say the least, abominable behavior. I just can't do it.

As it is now, if Mother forgives me, in the end she will have someone to take care of her. I don't trust my foot either, and in my case I need someone to take care of me.

We are sure of work until October in Sweden; the summer never presents any difficulty, and as soon as we get our passages together we will go home.

So far, so good. If you don't write to me again I shall understand. On the other hand I'd love to hear from you again.' [11]

Probably anticipating the effect this latest turnaround would have on Mrs. Casely-Hayford and her relationship with her daughter, Anna Graves tried to persuade Gladys to change her mind again by warning her about some of the unexpected misfortunes that might prevent 'Big Boy' from giving her the kind of support she needed, or from giving her talents an opportunity to develop. She went so far as to warn Gladys that 'Big Boy' might even die, which would leave her unable to achieve all that she could by improving her education. Anna Graves concluded her letter by saying that if the pair really loved each other, they could surely trust each other in a separation of eight months. She must have thought she had handled a delicate matter with the utmost tact but to Gladys she sounded too much like her mother to be trusted as a sympathetic mediator any longer.

Gladys does not reply to that letter for a month, by which time she is installed at Ruskin College having traveled via Berlin, and from there to London, where she spent a week nursing her brother, Archie, who was in England on business and had fallen ill with malaria. In the end, she arrived in Oxford only a few days after the beginning of term.[12]

---OOOIIIOOO---

It is hard to imagine that Mrs. Casely-Hayford played no part in finally getting Gladys to Ruskin, especially after she told Anna Graves the August before,

'I have quite made up my mind that she shall go to Ruskin in September.' [13]

Yet Anna Graves receives the following letter from her, dated just two days earlier than Gladys's:

'Thank you so much for your sweet lovely letter of condolence, which arrived by the last steamer. It is no use hiding the fact that at the time the blow was a knockout one, to say nothing of my poor little girl's callous, heartless, utterly selfish indifference to my welfare. Thank God, however, now it is nothing but a bad dream. On September 29th I received a cable from her, "Proceeding to Ruskin" so my heart is at rest. What has brought about this change of attitude I do not yet know. I believe your letter to her had a great deal to do with it, coupled perhaps, with the appalling economic state of Germany just at present. I believe many theatres have smashed up. They were faced with a winter of unemployment. Anyway, whatever it is, Gladys has come to her senses, so I can only sing a Doxology.'[14]

Gladys's explanation is rather different:

'Strangely enough it was B.B. who, knowing nothing of your letters, told me that I must not give up College for marriage – that I must wait till he could take care of me.' [15]

Her first impressions of Ruskin seem to have been quite favourable, however, for the same letter continues,

'I have been here five days now and seem to have crammed an enormous amount into a very short space. My curriculum consists of literature, drawing (at the Ruskin School of Drawing) and German. I think I might as well turn up my German to good account: to read and write it with the facility with which I speak will always help me to get good jobs. The spirit of Ruskin is delightful and I feel quite at home.' [16]

But her next letter sounds more subdued.

'There is far too much to do here – no time for outside things at all. My foot is giving me no end of trouble. I have had to cut down all outside lectures. My progress is slow, or rather intermittent – owing to this physical handicap. My tutors, on the whole do not seem dissatisfied at all, neither am I setting the Thames on fire. As regards Ruskin being stodgy: it is extremely interesting – quite the contrary. The students are really nice and I like them all. I think they like me.' [17]

More information about Gladys's progress at Ruskin is contained in another letter from her mother to Anna Graves. That December, Mrs. Casely-Hayford writes,

'I know you rejoice with me that Gladys is now at Ruskin where she has settled down very happily and seems to be making friends and getting on so well. Gandhi visited the College and she got him to autograph her book of poems*. At recent lecture on Schumann, for which a chairman had to be elected by vote, her fellow students elected her, and Mr. Barrett Brown writes to say she presided very well.

I am doing my best now to send her a little more money, so that she can have a little electric stove in her room, and get a taxi for her lectures, because she says the steps are so trying – she is 4 flights up – so that she is completely done by the time the day is over.' [18]

Anna Graves also received news of Gladys, this time with more detailed information, from the principal of Ruskin College, Mr. Barratt Brown:

'We have very much enjoyed having her with us, and she is exceedingly popular with the students and very happy here. Gladys has been taking drawing lessons with the Ruskin Master of Drawing, Albert Rutherson, and also some English and German. I have been very much impressed with her capacity for writing both prose and verse, and find that she picks up very quickly points of technique and sees where she has gone wrong. She has been somewhat handicapped by her infirmity, and I have arranged for her to have a ground floor room close by the College with a fire, as she has been worried both by the amount of stair climbing and the cold.

She is a most delightful person to help. I can see a clash coming some day between her own ambitions in the directions of writing or making the collection of African folk tales and drama, and her mother's natural desire to have her in her own school. The solution will depend very much on her own progress and capacity for actual achievement. I conceive that it might be a good thing if she could have a second year here to complete her training both in drawing and writing.'[19]

Tragically, that did not happen, for just over two months later, Anna Graves received another, very different, letter from Mr. Barratt Brown. Sounding much more formal on this occasion, he wrote,

'I believe that Miss Sidgwick has already written to you telling you of the unfortunate breakdown of Miss Casely-Hayford. I am glad to say that she is making very good progress, and it does not appear to be more than an acute case of hysteria. It was, however, a very anxious time, but I managed to get her into a private mental nursing home as a voluntary patient, and I have had a cable from her mother that a relative will arrive early in April, when she will, I hope, be well enough to go home.'[20]

---OOOIIIOOO---

A closer scrutiny of Gladys's letters to Anna Graves in the preceding three months gives the reader considerable insight into her state of mind as she left Germany for England. First of all, there are the letters themselves: they are much shorter than before and, though they still end with affection, sound somewhat distant now, polite rather than friendly, as if Gladys no longer believes that Anna Graves is on her side. Secondly, there is the information the letters contain – giving as one of her reasons for staying longer in Europe the need to buy a new winter coat when, in her letter dated July 21, 1931, she has told Anna Graves that she has a good one; her several references to the trouble her leg is giving her. She must also have complained about her leg to her mother and Mr. Barratt Brown because they both mention it in their own recent letters to Anna Graves. This is significant because Beth Torrey, with whom Anna Graves corresponded over Gladys's illness, remarked that Gladys could always do more with her leg when she wanted to or was interested than she could when she was bored, or did not want to do the thing being asked of her. Indeed, Gladys had *danced* on that leg for three months, though it is possible that her illness in Berlin had left it further impaired.

Ruefully describing 'Big Boy' saying she should not forgo college for marriage as 'strange' is another significant bit of information. It must have been a severe blow to hear him almost repeating Anna Graves's arguments. She also tells Anna Graves that she had to delay her arrival at Ruskin for a whole week in order to nurse Archie through malaria – Archie who, when she was struggling to survive in Germany, had, according to one of her letters, sent her just one pound in two years. [21] (I might be misinterpreting this last, however, since Gladys's capacity for love and kindness was, according to her mother, 'outstanding') [22]. Finally, there is the style of her writing which I now found abrupt and almost disjointed, compared with her previously free-flowing paragraphs.

These clues suggested to me that, as in the case of going to Columbia, Gladys had never truly committed herself to going for further studies. She had merely resigned herself to doing so under the pressure piled on her by her mother, Anna Graves and, to her great dismay, by 'Big Boy' himself. Even while trying to get on with her work during that first term, she had probably remained deeply unhappy. She successfully hid her feelings from her mother, her tutors and her fellow students, but must have been concealing anguish all along.

Chapter Seven

Shattered Hopes

WHEN news of Gladys's breakdown reached her Anna Graves wondered with feelings of guilt whether, in her desire to help both mother and daughter, she had perhaps done more harm than good.[1] By contrast, Mrs. Casely-Hayford does not seem to have considered whether any actions of hers might have contributed to making Gladys so ill. She expressed the view that the breakdown had probably been caused by Gladys's 'music, literature and drawing, all bursting to express themselves at the same time, coupled with her unfortunate love affair...' and thought some bad news about 'Big Boy' might have triggered it.[2]

She was probably right, regarding the possibility of some bad news about 'Big Boy' being the trigger; for after having some searching conversations with Gladys, Mr. Barratt Brown wrote to tell Anna Graves that he thought the double strain of the conflict with her mother and the love affair in Germany, *which now seemed to be over*, were probably what had caused her breakdown, rather than any strain imposed by her work. [3] Gladys might have contemplated a future without 'Big Boy' and one in which, after Ruskin, she would have to return to the life she had hoped to escape for good – living and working in her mother's shadow. That thought must have been more than she could bear.

She enters Warneford Hospital, a private nursing home, voluntarily. Her first visitors were her cousin, Dr. Charles Easmon and his wife, who were living temporarily in Edinburgh while he attended a course. The Easmons did not think she was all that ill because she spoke to them quite normally, though she seemed very apathetic about her surroundings. Charles Easmon wrote to tell Anna Graves that in his opinion, Gladys ought to be well enough in a month's time to travel home without a special attendant, though a companion would be necessary.[4] In less than a month, however, he wrote Anna Graves again to say that Warneford Hospital had informed him that unless Gladys could be sent home quickly, compulsory committal to a psychiatric hospital would be necessary because she was not improving.[5] It later emerged that the sense of urgency conveyed by that message from the hospital was due, not so much to concern about Gladys's lack of progress towards recovery, as to objections raised by other inmates to having a 'mulatto' in their midst. [6]

Anna Graves was Gladys's next visitor. Though she found the gardens and general environment at Warneford beautiful and the attendant seemed kind enough, she became convinced that Gladys was not receiving the right treatment because she seemed heavily sedated. Indeed, during the visit, Gladys put her head on the table and apparently fell sound asleep. Anna Graves brought up the matter of Gladys's treatment with Mr. Barratt Brown who agreed that she would be better off at the Oxford County Mental Hospital, Littlemore. The obstacle to her being transferred there was the need for compulsory committal for which he refused to take sole responsibility, and so far, Mrs. Casely-Hayford had withheld her consent. Once again, Anna Graves intervened and within a short time, had obtained the necessary authorisation from Mrs. Casely-Hayford through Charles Easmon. [7]

Gladys is committed to the psychiatric hospital under the signatures of Mr. Barratt Brown and Anna Graves. In her notes Anna Graves describes the experience as extremely painful and frightening, especially when she realised that discharge from compulsory admission would depend entirely on the hospital authorities. She only felt better about it when Dr. Goode, the chief psychiatrist, assured herself and Mr. Barratt Brown that Gladys would not be kept in hospital one day longer than was absolutely necessary.[8]

---OOOIIIOOO---

Gladys enters Littlemore early in June 1932. Just three weeks later, her condition has undergone such a remarkable improvement that I wonder whether her illness would have lasted over four months had she received appropriate treatment right from the start. According to Anna Graves, having obtained a summary history of Gladys's life from her, Dr. Goode came to the following conclusion as to the psychological causes of her breakdown:

'Her mother does not love her. Neither the mother nor the child knows this consciously, but sub-consciously they do. The subconscious knowledge which the mother has of her feelings towards the child makes her persuade herself that she has a special affection and she shows it in indulgence and, since she is autocratic by nature, interfering 'concern'. Her rankling resentment against her husband, though, is so great that she does not, or so I diagnose the case, feel the love she likes to think she has for the child who is so much like him. Gladys, also subconsciously, feels she has not her mother's real affection, craves it, and tries to win it by arousing pity, hence her having formed a habit of making the most of her affliction. She is also very much attracted by her mother, admires her greatly and feels her magnetic influence strongly; but at the same time fears doing what her mother wants her to do lest she should lose the power of being herself, knowing - sub-consciously - that her real self is something her mother cannot understand, since it is so much her father; and also being conscious and also sub-conscious of her mother's tremendous will-power and of her mother's influence over her, this fear has grown and grown until it has produced a defense mania...' [9]

While assuring the reader of her notes that what she has written is only an approximation of Dr. Goode's psychoanalysis, Anna Graves puts those remarks between quotation marks, suggesting that they are almost his exact words. Yet one cannot help wondering how much of that analysis actually originated from Dr. Goode and how much from her own mind. How, for instance, would Dr. Goode have known that Gladys was 'so much like her father', unless Anna Graves told him so? Yet she herself had never met Mr. Casely Hayford and must have heard of this similarity only from his estranged wife, and probably at a time when Mrs. Casely-Hayford was feeling particularly exasperated by Gladys's behaviour. Besides, though Dr. Goode would certainly have been guided in his questioning of Gladys by the information provided by Anna Graves, I find it quite surprising that he would have been so unethical as to go into the details of his clinical evaluation with someone who was not a member of the family, even though she had been one of the signatories to Gladys's compulsory admission. Mr. Barratt Brown's brief letter to Anna Graves seems a more accurate account of what Dr. Goode must have reported to them:

'that he had had some very thorough and straight forward talks with Gladys and, as a result, concluded that she was a manic depressive.' [10]

Very soon after her admission to Littlemore, Dr. Goode gets Gladys to teach raffia work to some of the other patients as occupational therapy. He also allows her out several times – on one occasion to buy raffia with the matron, and on another with Mr. Barratt Brown who takes her for a drive with a couple of other students. Mr. Barratt Brown finds her very reticent and depressed during that first outing, which he attributes partly to shyness about meeting people after the trouble she caused, and partly to a certain amount of natural fear about the future. He finds it strange that she refuses to talk either about Dr. Goode or about her mother, and is touched when she says in parting, "I am going to try." On another occasion, Gladys is allowed to go back to the college by herself for tea with the matron and some of her fellow students.[11] When she returns to Littlemore, she sits down at the piano and plays beautifully.

Meanwhile, her mother had characteristically put the distressing situation into the hands of God. She told Anna Graves,

> 'At first Gladys's breakdown was a terrible blow to me, but of late I have been so extraordinarily sustained by the 'exceeding greatness of His Power' and by the 'exceeding riches of His Grace,' that my faith in Him makes me perfectly sure that she is on the royal road to recovery.' [12]

It was partly for this reason that she had refused to have Gladys committed earlier, and also from a parent's natural reluctance to take such drastic action, knowing that the stigma of a mental illness would haunt Gladys for the rest of her life. She had been trying to raise money to go over to England to bring Gladys home herself, but her lack of success in doing so up to that point convinced her that God had not provided the money because the journey was unnecessary.[13] However, by the time Gladys entered the hospital, Charles Easmon had come into an unexpected windfall which made it possible for her to make the trip after all. She now concluded that God wanted her to bring Gladys home and wrote announcing her imminent arrival,[14] rather to the dismay of Dr. Goode. He was by this time convinced of the major role Mrs. Casely-Hayford had played in causing Gladys's mental turmoil and would have preferred her to stay away until her daughter had fully recovered. [15]

Mrs. Casely-Hayford arrived about a month after Gladys's admission at Littlemore, and was 'very agreeably surprised to see [her] darling daughter,' whom she woke from a doze with a kiss. Gladys, for whom her mother's arrival is a complete surprise, is bewildered at first but tears of joy soon start streaming down her face. She hugs her mother fiercely but refuses to speak, which Mrs. Casely-Hayford puts down to 'sheer cussedness.' [16]

Parts of Mrs. Casely-Hayford's letters describing her visit to Oxford clearly reveal her domineering character. For instance, not knowing that Dr. Goode had already occupied Gladys with teaching raffia work, she told Anna Graves that she thought it was high time her daughter had some employment because sitting and brooding all day was not good for her – as if a specialist in mental illness would not have realised that and taken appropriate action. [17] In another letter, she wrote about interviewing the doctor and of having a searching talk with him, not the other way round, as one would expect; and then she dismissed his comments,

> '...in one breath he told me I had spoilt Gladys, and then in another, told me she was afraid of me. He told me that Gladys had had her own way, and had therefore not exercised her powers of self-control, etc.' [18]

Further into that consultation, Dr. Goode had sent for Gladys, questioned her again and asked if she wanted to return home. At first Gladys said a definite 'No,' though she would not give any reason for her refusal. Mrs. Casely-Hayford, however, had no doubt whatsoever about the reason for her daughter's reluctance to return to Freetown, and gave Anna Graves her opinion in her usual forthright manner:

> 'After three years residence in Europe, she is going back a failure, in spite of her pronounced ability and she is ashamed.

Had she followed my advice things would have been very different.' [19]

Gladys later agrees for her mother to book their passage home since Dr. Goode is quite ready to discharge her. Her formal release has to wait another three weeks until the next meeting of the hospital board, contradicting Dr. Goode's earlier assurance that she will not be kept in hospital one day more than is absolutely necessary. Meanwhile, Mrs. Casely-Hayford remained in Oxford and spent as much time with Gladys as she could. She ended the letter,

> 'Oh Miss Graves how wonderful God is !!!! As far as I can see, Gladys is just a little eccentric. At times she is absent-minded, and she also has fits of depression, which I am sure will disappear as time goes on, and sometimes she is not as polite as I would like her to be. But her conversation is most interesting and full of sparkling wit…Oh Miss Graves, I am amazed at the marvellous progress she has made towards recovery and all I can do is to sing a Doxology… As far as I can see Gladys is returning home to help me, of her own free will. I have not said a word to her on the subject, but I can see how things are moving.' [20]

She had obviously learned no lessons from the crisis, and was still refusing to entertain any suggestion that her daughter did not want to work with her.

Gladys and her mother sail for home shortly afterwards, but it is not a restful voyage for Gladys is still in a highly nervous state and the strange faces and hustle and bustle at the different ports at which the ship calls bother her unduly. On their arrival in Freetown, Mrs. Casely-Hayford therefore thought it wise to send her with an attendant to a house in the country for another month of rest and recuperation while she returned to work. [21]

Today Gladys would be described as having a bipolar disorder which, with its dramatic mood swings, is apparently not unusual among individuals of a highly artistic temperament.[22] However, assuming that Dr. Goode's diagnosis was correct, hers seems to have been a relatively mild case, since there was probably no specific medication to control its symptoms in the early 1930s and I have unearthed no evidence that she ever suffered another major breakdown. However, several months after their return to Freetown, her mother wrote to tell Anna Graves that she was still extremely short-tempered and continued to show signs of absentmindedness, lack of concentration and eccentricity. It also seems that even after she had recovered well enough to pick up the threads of her life again, she had to leave Freetown periodically for the peace and quiet of more rural surroundings;[23] and she made several trips to her family in the Gold Coast, which might have been related to a need for a complete change of environment from time to time.

Chapter Eight

Taking up the threads of life again

BOTH Gladys and her mother next write to Anna Graves on the same day, November 16, 1932 – two months after their return from England. As usual, they are responding to letters from Anna Graves. Gladys must have written at her mother's suggestion, for her letter is quite brief and hurriedly done in pencil because, she says, her pen is up another flight of steps (her painful leg, obviously still a factor). She tells Anna Graves that she has started doing portraits in water colour; and she must have something of a social life because she is about to rush off to a tea party. One paragraph of her letter, however, contains two pieces of information which Anna Graves must have read with a sigh:

> 'Mother wants me to be head of her school. I would rather go to Achimota if possible. Of course, there is still Big Boy somewhere in the background. I am terribly worried because I have not heard from him for some time.'

Her letter ends on this rather pathetic note:

> 'I don't seem to be able to fit in to home life here at all: but I'm trying my best. Nobody can take Big Boy's place you see.'[1]

Mrs. Casely-Hayford, on the other hand, went into some detail about Gladys's progress and present life:

> 'My dear daughter is almost her old self again – indeed to the casual eye, she is perfectly all right, but it is only when you

live with her that her lack of concentration, and little idiosyncrasies are apparent. But our prayers have been so marvellously answered, that I am quite confident she will be perfectly herself before the Festival Season... At this moment she is going out to finish a painting of an African boy which reflects great credit on her art... For the last fortnight I have been down with a serious attack of fever. I can assure you I have never had a more able nurse.' [2]

Anna Graves had probably made some anxious inquiries in her own letter regarding Gladys and the sensitive subject of her working at the school because the letter continues,

'Of course she does not go down to the school, although if nothing else turns up she will be willing to help me for a short time every day. I think she was very frightened when she saw how ill I was, and that has given her a greater sense of filial duty than anything else so far. I expect in another year she will be down at Achimota, but for the present getting her hand in here won't hurt her a bit.' [3]

Almost a year goes by before Mrs. Casely-Hayford wrote to Anna Graves again:

'With other people Gladys is absolutely natural, except for a quick temper and sometimes lack of self control. With me, however, when we are alone, she does display moods and tenses (sic), because she still has it at the back of her mind that I frustrated her marriage. I have suffered quite a lot of heartbreak at her treatment of me. But even that is infinitely better than it was...

Of her own free will she helps me in the School and is now undergoing a correspondence course in Drawing so as to get a Diploma which will enable her to become a qualified Drawing Master. She has also taken up the thread of her writing again, and is now busy on a play in commemoration of the Centenary of William Wilberforce's death – which we shall celebrate in October when the weather is fine – and which will be produced then. Three months ago she put on one of her old plays in order to raise funds for the school and received the heartiest congratulations of the whole community, from the Governor downwards.' [4]

After another year, she wrote again:

'I am sure you will be delighted to know that she is ever so much more rational and though she is still eccentric she puts in a great deal of useful work. She has been commissioned to write a weekly Children's Page for one of the local papers, and her powers of concentration are gradually returning…My great trouble is her unreasonable obstinacy. She takes all her work and shuts it up in a drawer and wild horses will not move her to send it out into the world and try its luck. This is, of course, all the harder, when we are so badly off, and when she cannot contribute a penny towards her upkeep. But it is simply a matter of patience, and in due season, if we faint not, we shall reap our reward.' [5]

The old pattern of parental pressure about her writing had obviously started again, but Gladys was no longer giving in to it. Though Mrs. Casely-Hayford put that down to 'unreasonable obstinacy', I believe that Gladys decided to take charge of her own work and not allow her mother to seek publication on her behalf any more.

Gladys herself writes to Anna Graves that same year – her second letter since returning home – and confirms what her mother has reported. She has taken up journalism again:

'I write a Children's Page regularly for one of our papers. I give them a Nature Study Course, some Craft Work – how to make a doll or a basket etc. – some topical Question of interest and a Book Review. Last week I did Dickens: the children He Wrote About... I give a few music lessons. School has just opened again. The worry of opening always upsets Mother. Fortunately we have a holiday on Monday, which gives us a long weekend in which to recuperate.

I am becoming an expert doughnut maker. These I sell at tea-time. It ekes out the pin money.

I don't go much to social functions. I have neither the energy nor time.
I have to prepare my lessons for the week, nurse Mother and get ready to recite Broken English [6] at Church tonight...Everyone is now doing double work on half pay, and we are all getting a little more cynical, more selfish and more overworked...'

It seems that she has not totally escaped working at the school after all; but she is increasingly doing more of what she finds personally fulfilling – either putting on shows or participating in them. The *Sierra Leone Weekly News* of September 9, 1933 has this note under Social Events:

'Concert at Wilberforce Memorial Hall under the patronage of Acting Governor and Mrs. Cookson. Miss Gladys Hayford's original readings created a great deal of merriment.'

I found no evidence that Gladys completed her Diploma in Drawing, but on the other hand, no evidence that she did not.

However, the idea of her going to work at Achimota School seems to have been quietly dropped.

---OOOIIIOOO---

In 1935, Mrs. Hayford's health broke down once again and this time she decided to seek treatment in England. Gladys seems to have reconciled herself to the loss of 'Big Boy' with the passage of time, and consequently her social life has improved. Soon after her mother's departure, she attends a party at the home of one of her closest friends, Mrs. Agnes Smythe-Macaulay. Mrs. Smythe-Macaulay, who was one of Dr. Cromwell's informants, told her that it was at this party that Gladys met the next man in her life – and her future husband – Arthur Hunter, [7] who was eight years her junior. [8]

Had Gladys wanted to hurt her mother, she could hardly have chosen a better way to do it. Like Nicholas Ballanta, Arthur Hunter came from Kissy Village, but unlike Ballanta, seems not to have had any education beyond secondary school. He was also quite dark in complexion (if that was indeed a negative factor with Mrs. Casely-Hayford). The attraction seems to have been their mutual love of ballroom dancing and their great compatibility on the dance floor. One of their favourite tunes was a hit of the day called *Wagon Wheels*, and so fond did they become of the melody that they whistled its first few bars when calling out to each other. [9] The romance blossomed rapidly; thoroughly smitten, Arthur Hunter tattooed 'Gladys' on one of his forearms, using the corrosive oil obtained from the skin of cashew nuts.[10]

Knowing how her mother would react to this new love affair, Gladys perhaps encouraged Arthur Hunter to propose or even proposed marriage herself before Mrs. Casely-Hayford returned from England. The wedding was kept a secret because most of the people close to Gladys disapproved of Arthur Hunter. An informant told me that she dressed for her wedding in the women's lavatory at the Victoria Park in the centre of Freetown. Family history has it that her cousin, Dr. Charles Easmon, somehow got wind of their plans and tried to put a stop to the ceremony, but by the time he discovered where it was taking place, Gladys and Arthur Hunter had become husband and wife – just two weeks after they met, according to Anna Graves.

The news of Gladys's marriage must have been another terrible blow to Mrs. Casely-Hayford. Indeed, after she returned home, she wrote to Anna Graves with unconcealed regret,

'She has chosen a man of very humble circumstances, indifferent education and no status whatsoever.'

However, she seems to have accepted the situation with good grace in the end, for the letter goes on,

'there seems to be such perfect understanding between them. In spite of their dire poverty they are showing such splendid courage, such fine contentment, such optimism, that I am quite sure the God whom they glorify will help them through. The man is thoroughly decent, clean, honest and devoted to his wife, and she reciprocates his affection with all her heart and soul, so that whenever they are on their feet I am sure all will be well, since they are building on such a sure foundation.' [11]

Later that same year she wrote to Anna Graves again,

'She and her man understand each other so well, and he has just got a post as a bus conductor which brings in a little and helps to keep the home fires burning. I never hear any grumbling, and I think they are really learning to lean upon God as their staunch ally.' [12]

Anna Graves sent the couple a wedding present of a "practical" nature, and both Gladys and her husband wrote separately to thank her for it. We have no record of Arthur Hunter's letter, but this is Gladys's, incidently, her last published letter to Anna Graves:

'I really feel very ashamed of myself for not having written to you before; but since my honeymoon my health has been precarious; our financial affairs ditto, so there has been no time for correspondence.

Yes, Arthur is very nice, as you will see from his letter to you, also. Your wedding present was a Godsend. Thank you very much indeed.

We are living in a small flat quite near Mother. There is a garage business below; which is lively, usually noisy and always interesting. Running the flat leaves very little time over for anything else. If I get stronger after Christmas I'll run another "show" – a revue, I think, this time.'

She has got her husband interested in music, for she continues,

'Hubby is sight-reading "The Merry Peasant" by Schumann, and I have been jumping up at intervals to supervise the boy and lay the breakfast table overnight.

There is no family yet. God's time is best.................

We have been married a year now, and still find matrimony satisfactory.' [13]

In her own letters after the marriage, Mrs. Casely-Hayford wrote of the couple being a financial burden on her; but one wonders whether she did indeed have to keep them going financially or whether she had taken it upon herself to meddle in their affairs. Gladys was obviously earning money through various pursuits. In her letter she mentioned laying the breakfast table overnight, which suggests having to make an early start in the morning. They also had a servant, which one would have thought an extravagance if they were that poor. Gladys also mentioned running "another show", suggesting that she earned money from this source from time to time, and her husband does not seem to have been unemployed for more than six months, if ever.

The Hunters are married for more than three years before they are blessed with a child. During Gladys's pregnancy they go to the Gold Coast where she seems to have spent weeks in hospital. In one version of her memoirs (quoted by Dr Cromwell), Mrs. Casely-Hayford describes an incident which took place while Gladys was admitted at Korle-Bu Hospital in Accra:

'In November 1939, she was lying in the very spacious and comfortable maternity ward at Korle-Bu Hospital, Accra, expecting her baby, when a terrible earthquake shook the town. It was about 7 o'clock in the evening and lasted only two or three minutes, but in all that time hell seemed to be let loose. The electricity gave out and in the pitch darkness, those poor women began to scream and shriek for help, as the furniture careered around the ward. Two of them gave birth at once, and above the pandemonium Gladys's clear voice rang out as she called on the women to pray. By the time she had finished, the frenzied shrieking and yelling had subsided, and calm was restored; the lights went on and peace descended on them all.' [14]

Writing her memoirs when she was an old woman, Mrs. Casely-Hayford must have had a lapse of memory because, according to records, the 1939 earthquake in Accra happened on June 22. This suggests that Gladys was in hospital for a prenatal rest rather than to give birth; her baby, a boy named Kobina Arthur Sydney, did not arrive until December 5, 1939.

Arthur Hunter once described to me, with fond amusement, Gladys's fumbling attempts to bathe Kobina for whom she wrote this charming little poem:

Baby Cobna*

Brown Baby Cobna, with his large black velvet eyes,
His little "cooes" of ecstacy, his gurgles of surprise.
With brass bells upon his ankles that laugh where'ere he goes,
It is rare for bells to tinkle above brown dimpled toes.

Brown Baby Cobna is so precious that we fear
Something might come and steal him, when we grown ups
are not near.
So we tied bells on his ankles, and kissed on to them this
charm:-
"Bells keep our Baby Cobna from all devils, and all harm."

Kobina (the Fante name given to boys born on a Tuesday), is usually called 'Kohbi' for short by Sierra Leoneans and 'Kobby' by Ghanaians, since it is correctly pronounced 'Kobna'.

The Hunter family return to Freetown some time after Kobina's birth, and for once the adult Gladys has brought her mother unqualified joy.

In January 1942, Mrs. Casely-Hayford wrote to Anna Graves,

'She [Gladys] has given me a darling little grandson… so extraordinarily intelligent and interesting that he fills my heart with joy and rejuvenates my poor, old, worn out frame.' [15]

Indeed, Kobina remembers that between his mother and grandmother he was enfolded in love all the time. Gladys made up this little song, which he has never forgotten:

Kobna Sydney, O where are you hiding,
Come out, I'll be chiding,
Come out very soon.

Don't you know Mother has plenty to do,
She can't spend all day just looking for you.

Kobna Sydney, O where are you hiding
Come out, I'll be chiding;
Come out very soon.

There were, however, darkening clouds over the horizon of his mother's life of which Kobina was blissfully unaware. In her penultimate letter to Anna Graves, having once again mentioned the great financial burden her daughter's marriage had put on her, Mrs. Casely-Hayford reported that Gladys started a café for the armed forces some time after the outbreak of the Second World War – apparently without the assistance of her husband. [16]

'[it] would have been a great success if she had only allowed me to have a finger in the management, which was quite beyond her. So it failed…'

'At the present moment I have taken a house for her at Wilberforce (at the time a rural hilltop village), where she can vegetate and where the salubrious air and restful surroundings will do her a world of good.' [17]

In November 1942, Mrs. Casely-Hayford wrote her last published letter to Anna Graves, giving her the information that:

'Gladys and her "Babbie" left us a week ago to visit her father's relatives down the Coast. I expect they will be there for a while.' [18]

The letter gave Anna Graves no further details, but I suspect that Gladys was traveling alone on this occasion because her marriage had broken down. This might also explain why she had tried to run a café single-handed, and why its failure had been such a devastating blow that she had to retire to the country for a while. She might have been trying to cope with the anguish of a broken marriage and the running of a business at the same time.

Why the Hunters went from 'splendid courage', 'perfect understanding', 'fine contentment' and 'such optimism' to a failed marriage must remain something of a mystery. Dr. Cromwell cites a family friend who told her that Arthur Hunter began to drink, became physically abusive and started a relationship with another woman.[19] However, Gladys's volatile temperament and her mother's interfering nature might also have played a part in souring their relationship, not to mention the couple's great difference in background and education.

It is quite possible that it was in order to pick up the pieces of her life yet again that Gladys decided to go down to the Gold Coast for an indefinite period. Kobina was almost three when they left Freetown. His first recollection of seeing his father was a chance encounter when he was five or six years old, so they were probably away for a couple of years.

They met his father on a Freetown street. Gladys merely introduced him, saying, "Kobby, this is your father."

"Good afternoon, Sir," Kobina remembers replying, to which his father answered, " Don't call me, Sir, call me 'Daddy'."

He recalls that he could not bring himself to do so on that occasion. However, like his six younger siblings, he eventually began to call his father, 'Papa', and they became good friends.

Kobina clearly remembers some of the adventures he shared with his mother while they lived in Accra [20] – going to open air cinemas and afterwards eating delicious snacks and drinking hot cocoa prepared and purchased by the wayside, having to hold on tight to his mother's skirts as they walked through the bustling markets, getting into trouble when he threw a stone at the window of a bus and cracked it, and even being carried from one train station to another because he had scrupulously obeyed his mother's instructions not to abandon their luggage. On his insistence, he was loaded into the baggage room with their bags and had to be rescued at the next station following a cabled message.

Although it is undated, Gladys perhaps wrote the following poem with its implied mother-son conversation as they returned to Freetown after that sojourn in the Gold Coast:

In Harbour (Freetown)

Oh wake up, do wake up, the land is in sight,
Slipping into the circle of sea and daylight.
Look slippy, my boy, the red glimmer of day
Will flush the horizon, whilst boats leave the bay.
You've your ears to be washed, and your teeth to
Your hair to be combed, and your shoes to be rubbed;
For there's Freetown in sight, and it never would do
For the land to feel half ashamed, sonny, of you.
Oh yes, there is breakfast – prayers need not be said?
Never heard of such nonsense, I'll send you to bed.
Why is Ma crying? Don't show such surprise,

It's the dew of old memories, awake in mine eyes.
There's Cape Lighthouse – King Tom, Lumley – home,
shore.
Did you say, sonny, Ma must not cry any more?

While they sailed into the Freetown harbour, her mind must have been full of poignant memories of a much happier homecoming with her husband and baby just a few years earlier.

Chapter Nine

Age did not wither her

BY the time Gladys and Kobina return to Freetown, Mrs. Casely-Hayford has retired and, for want of a suitable successor, reluctantly closed down the Girls' Vocational School. The family now share a house belonging to Dr. Charles Easmon at 2, Charlotte Street. Gladys's prayer that another way of securing her mother's future be found has been answered, for the property at 9, Gloucester Street, which Charles Easmon owns jointly with Mrs. Casely-Hayford, has been let, assuring her of a small but regular income.

Gladys's life now seems to have settled into a pattern of undertaking various pursuits to earn money of her own. As Kobina remembers it, they included working as a nursemaid with an Indian family, buying a treeful of mangoes from the Sierra Leone hinterland to sell in Freetown, and making soap on a small scale. He also retains a vivid memory of being put in charge of a pile of toy soldiers for sale on the pavement outside the house on Charlotte Street. Along with these ventures, as the spirit moves her, Gladys continues to put on her variety shows and plays either at the Wilberforce Memorial Hall, which used to be on the corner of Water (now Wallace-Johnson) Street and Gloucester Street,[1] or at the British Council hall (located at the time on the lower slope of Tower Hill, taken over first by the Paramount Hotel and more recently by the Ministry of Defense).

Most of her shows and plays either dealt with aspects of African life, or were familiar English stories, Africanised. She not only composed the music and songs for them, but also wrote their entire scripts. Kobina recalls her sometimes[2] even creating her own backdrops, and remembers being with her on the empty top floor of a building near their home where she was painting a scene on a huge piece of white cloth. I found only the merest fragments of one or two of Gladys's plays among her written work, and none of the music—a great pity because she seems to have become the cultural luminary in the Freetown of her day. According to one of Dr. Cromwell's informants, her shows and plays were so popular that 'everybody in Freetown who was anybody' attended them— "Europeans, Americans, Asiatics as well as Africans crowded the Wilberforce Hall for tickets and as Patrons". [3]

During this period of her life, Kobina recalls that Gladys somehow managed to build herself a small house at Wilberforce Village, though how she obtained the money to embark on such an ambitious project remains a complete mystery. Her father left her a house in the Gold Coast in his will. [4] It might have been sold and the proceeds used to acquire land and put up her own building; but this is pure speculation on my part.

One of my Stuart aunts told me that the first purchase Gladys made in connection with building her house was the lock for the front door, saying that having it would ensure that she finished the project. With the help of a snuff-loving labourer called Momoh, she did just that, working on the project until the house was completed and the front door lock in place. Kobina remembers spending days and nights with her on the building site, their temporary home a shack constructed from flattened oil drums. He also remembers sampling Momoh's snuff, which sent him reeling drunkenly into his mother's sympathetic embrace.

Gladys's reputation must have received a further boost when, in 1948, a selection of her poems, both in Krio and English, was published in Freetown in a small volume entitled Take um so.[5] Some time afterwards, she returns to the Gold Coast for another of her periodic visits. Kobina cannot remember why she left him behind on that occasion, but remembers her asking him what present he would like. Being an avid fan of action-packed movies featuring cowboys and indians, he requested a cowboy-style shirt. He also recalls how much he cried when they parted — as if he had a premonition that he would never see her again.

From what he remembers being told, Gladys took a teaching job in a town called Keta, on the Atlantic coast, in what is now the Volta Region of Ghana. There, she was struck down by an acute attack of malaria, developed the complication known as black water fever, and died a few days later. So her life ended where it began – in the Gold Coast. She passed away in the rainy season, but perhaps parts of the wish expressed in this poem were fulfilled:

A Dying Wish

My one wish when I'm dying and my body is sinking low,
Is to lie so my eyes can gaze on the green leaves that the winds blow,
And if I should go in the morning, I'd like the warm sky blue
With sunlight pouring its brilliant rays on tree-flowers filled with dew;
And if I should go at noontide, amidst its glowing heat,
I would like to hear the hum of bees and butterflies' greet;
And if I should go at even, I would that my dimming eyes
May rest on the lingering beauty of summer sunset skies.
And if I should go at nightfall, I would like to go when the air
Is wrapped in a mantle of purple, like a grand old prayer.
I wish to die in a garden, within the sound of rills,
Sky overhead, and grass beneath, and far in the distance – hills.

The Sierra Leone Daily Mail of Friday, 25th August, 1950 carried this brief obituary:

'It is with much regret that we report that the death occurred at Accra, Gold Coast, on Wednesday night of Miss Gladys May Casely-Hayford (whose married name was Mrs. Hunter). Miss Hayford who was 47 years old died after a short illness.

She was the daughter of the late Mr. Casely Hayford, M.C.L. M.B.E., Co-founder of the Congress of British West Africa, of Cape Coast and Mrs. A. Casely-Hayford, M.B.E. of Freetown'.

Some time after her death, Gladys's belongings were returned to Freetown. Among them was Kobina's present – a cowboy shirt.

In the mid-1950s, Kobina was sent to the Gold Coast to complete secondary school, and recalls that his uncle, Archie Casely-Hayford, showed him his mother's grave. However, sadly, we have so far been unable to find it at the Osu Cemetery in Accra where the remains of several other Casely-Hayfords, including her father and Archie himself are buried close together.

---OOOIIIOOO---

The announcement of a memorial service for Gladys, in which she was described as 'this illustrious lady', must have left Mrs. Casely-Hayford somewhat bewildered because she had hardly approved of her daughter once she became an adult. I would venture to say that it was the reaction of the Freetown community to the news of Gladys's death that made her mother start to review and revise her own opinion of her. Indeed, in her *Profile of Gladys*, which was written some time after Gladys passed away, she admits that,

'It was only at her death that I realized what a place she had made for herself in the affections of the community. I went to my window about two hours after the radio had announced her death in Accra, and saw a group of market women looking up at the house disconsolately and utterly woebegone.'[6]

On the whole, Mrs. Casely-Hayford's *Profile of Gladys* is a loving tribute to her daughter's memory, all the more affecting because she is writing about a someone with whom she had such a stormy relationship. The following passages show her kinder attitude:

'Even when she was about to be stricken down with her short fatal illness in 1950, she wrote us a letter which was full of jokes and fun, radiating her joyous personality.'

'Gladys was no respecter of persons and some of her guests were downright disreputable. As long as you were a human being in need, you could count on Gladys for help. Invariably, she brought home these lame dogs and I, with my meagre income, had to extend hospitality – sometimes quite grudgingly. She insisted that whatever we had must be shared. This outstanding capacity for love and kindness swallowed up her many eccentricities.

One day, she was walking along the thoroughfare near the market when she saw a man lying in the middle of the road. She pulled him to the kerb and seeing that he was still breathing, rushed into a shop for brandy and milk to revive him. By this time, quite a crowd had gathered, and one woman shouted out, " Nor make norbody tiff dah lili missis in poss oh! You nor see waitin e day do?' (Don't you dare steal this little woman's purse! She is doing a good deed.") Gladys then realized that she was carrying her bag under her arm, so she looked all round the crowd and spotted one man.

"Oh," she said, handing it to him. "Please take care of it for me." After her ministrations, the sick man revived and an ambulance came to take him off. The crowd dispersed and Gladys suddenly realized that she had parted with her hand-bag. The man was still standing there and came up to her at once. "Missis," he said, "Here is your bag." It transpired that this was a man, in and out of prison the whole time, but after the look of confidence and trust Gladys gave him, he admitted that he could not possibly steal from her.

Although there were times when I secretly felt that Gladys was inclined to be irreligious, I realize now how grossly I misjudged her. Whatever their appearance, she was everlastingly seeking for people's good qualities rather than condemning them. As Carlyle often pointed out, it is 'this gift of tenderness and understanding sympathy that gives the measure of our intellects.' Having definitely conquered fastidiousness, Gladys was a spiritual aristocrat.' [7]

However, after paying her daughter such a high compliment, Mrs. Casely-Hayford cannot resist listing some of her shortcomings for the reader:

'She had no sense of values and never could discriminate in any way, either with human beings or commodities. Then too, she utterly lacked determination and perseverance.' [8]

Perhaps she felt compelled to be totally frank and objective in her assessment of Gladys, but even from this distance in time, it saddens me to think that she was publicly critical of her only child who had died too young, and who had triumphed over adversity to accomplish much of which a parent could be proud. Perhaps that criticism arose from some lingering resentment that Gladys had not fulfilled her expectations of her. Also, bearing in mind that Mrs. Casely-Hayford fell seriously ill several times during her long life but always recovered, I am inclined to think that in her view, Gladys's death was yet another instance of her daughter's 'utter lack of determination.'

After reading the *Profile of Gladys* and her letters to Anna Graves, I was left with the impression that Mrs. Casely-Hayford assessed Gladys, to a large extent, in terms of her own unfulfilled hopes and dreams, but there could be other reasons for her attitude. For one thing, she had become deaf during the period of Gladys's second creative flowering as a musician and dramatist, and may therefore not have been fully aware of her daughter's activities and reputation. Besides, according to one of her letters to Anna Graves, Gladys became extremely secretive about her work and kept it locked up in a drawer.[9] She had probably been equally secretive about other aspects of her life.

It is not hard to imagine Mrs. Casely-Hayford complaining about Gladys's behaviour to other sympathetic listeners, and being urged to be more tolerant, knowing her daughter's instability. Having read Gladys's poetry and letters closely, however, I would argue against such an oversimplification of the matter. Although I am as unqualified to make psychoanalytic judgments as Anna Graves, I believe her mental state was the result not only of her bitterness towards her mother, but also of a conflict between her free-spirited nature and the standards imposed by her strict Christian upbringing and the conservative society in which she lived. This view is supported by a comment Mrs. Casely-Hayford made to Anna Graves in 1932: that she would have to find Gladys a husband because she had one of those natures that could not lead a life of 'single blessedness'.[10]

From my interpretation of the evidence available to me, it also seems clear that, despite Gladys's largely European education, a deep longing to be true to her patriotic vision of Africa and to identify with black people in general lay at the heart of much of her so-called eccentricity. Though light-skinned herself, she declared that black was beautiful years before it became one of the slogans of racial empowerment among African Americans. She also seems to have been attracted to dark-skinned African men, which might be one reason why she merely flirted with her ardent Afro-Caribbean suitor whom Anna Graves describes as 'a mulatto'. Gladys enjoyed associating with ordinary African people, choosing to endure the discomforts of traveling steerage on the coastal vessels even when she had enough funds for a second-class cabin, and trawling through markets herself, something probably unheard of among women of her social status in those days. According to one of my Stuart aunts, she sometimes tied wrappers around her waist like a 'native' woman. Dressing that way would certainly have caused a good deal of negative comment among Freetown's Creole élite for most of whom the height of civilisation at the time was to look as European as possible, at least in public.

I think that, having consciously embraced both her blackness and being African, Gladys wanted to use her gifts of mind and spirit to help make her own small corner of the continent the kind of place envisaged in this poem:

My African Hymn

Oh, land of tropic splendour engirded by the seas,
Whose forest-crested mountains lift heads unto the breeze;

May patriotism render its praise on sea and shore,
Till Africa, great Africa, becomes renowned once more.

May God walk on her mountains, and in her plains be peace.
May laughter fill her valleys, and may her sons increase;

Restored be strength and beauty and visions of the past;
Till Africa comes once again into her own at last.

Destroy race prejudices, break down the bars of old.
Let each man deem his brother of far more wealth than gold.

Till tribes be merged together, to form one perfect whole,
With Africa its beating pulse, and Africa its soul.

Oh, Lord as we pass onward, through evolution rise;
May we retain clear vision, that truth may light our eyes.
That joy and peace and laughter be ours, instead of tears,
Till Africa gains strength and calm, progressing through the years.

Indeed, it is possible that she always intended her musical and literary compositions to be primarily for the entertainment and inspiration of her own downtrodden and colonised people, hence her apparent lack of drive when it came to making a name for herself in Europe and America. Of course, that attitude, too, would have been considered highly eccentric by members of her family and social class.

Having 'listened' to various people who knew Gladys, and to Gladys herself, through her writing, I have drawn other tentative conclusions about her. One is that, unlike most of us, she never had to struggle hard within herself to 'conquer' fastidiousness. She seems either to have been blessed from birth with a high level of spiritual awareness, or to have advanced rapidly in that direction as she grew older. This must have been what her mother sensed quite early on when she described her personality as 'ethereal' and later in the *Profile of Gladys* as that of 'a spiritual aristocrat'. Indeed, people of such enlightened consciousness are no respecters of persons, which would explain why Gladys inspired such affection within all levels of society in Freetown and probably in the Gold Coast as well; from all accounts, she never put on airs.

Her spirituality comes through in many of her poems; in the following hymn, for instance,

A Prayer

Change thou my heart, O God,
Until that spark divine
Re-animates each hidden part,
To make my heart like Thine.
That through my darkest hours of life,
Some light may shine.

Change neither lot nor circumstance,
Life's worry, pain or smart,
Change neither time nor space, but oh
Change Thou my heart,
So that I see in everything
Thy counterpart.

* Written aged twenty-three

in this rueful reflection;

Inspiration

God always whips me first,
Then hands me a poem for consolation;
Wrought out of my punishment,
Metered by forgiveness,
Rhymed by His love.

and again, in this rapturous outpouring of praise:

The Glorious World

O Lord, what a glorious world You have made:
What a beautiful, wonderful world,
With its hills and its valleys, its plains and its mountains,
Blue heavens above them unfurled.

Oh, the flaring, brave, glorious chant of Thy blossoms;
The joyful sweet notes of a bird in the tree;
The gold skirts of earth, and the crest of the billows;
Thy pines and Thy palms, and Thy oaks, and Thy willows
Are marvellous things to see!

I also believe that, having come to terms with the knowledge
that she could never live up to her mother's standards and
expectations, Gladys took Anna Graves's advice to let
recriminations 'run off her like water off a duck's back',[11] and
lived in a way that was true to her own ideals and aspirations
which could perhaps be summed up in this untitled poem:

There's nothing like using the things that God gives you,
Use up to the last dregs, the cup of your lives.
 Boys, grow up and live to be stalwart, good fathers,
And girls, just live up to being real Christian wives.
Use your hands and your feet, and your lips for the speaking
Of things that are noble, pure, honest and true.
With your hearts for the anvils that nations are built on,
To build up the Africa destined for you.

There's nothing like using the things that God gives you,
Use, learn in the process of using, your eyes,
That they may see beauty, and wisdom, and nature,
Hope, evil, sin, pity, and Heaven, curved skies.
Use your eyes as the pools where your soul should be shining,

As a beacon for those who are standing apart,
From the call of the fatherhood, brotherhood, sympathy,
Of the great yearning love in old Africa's heart.

There's nothing like using the things that God
gives you,
Use, so that it echoes o'er the mountains, your voice.
Lifted high above earth and its sordid realities,
To the plains of Belief, with the glad cry, "Rejoice".
Use, your heart, mind and soul, let them ring through your
crying,
That God works for good, and His mercy shall stand,
As streams interlacing the plains with the mountains,
In rivers and fountains, throughout our dear land.

From the evidence to hand, much of it provided by her
harshest critic, in my opinion, Gladys Casely-Hayford well
deserved the epithet, 'this illustrious lady' used in the
announcement of her memorial service in Freetown. In spite of
her frailties and the trials and tribulations of her own life which, I
came to learn, included an operation for breast cancer, she used
her talents to enrich and uplift the lives of others, not for
financial gain but for the soul satisfaction it gave her to do so. She
wrote hundreds of poems of varying lengths and complexity,
many of which, as her mother observed are '...a joy and
inspiration to read.' By retelling traditional folk tales in public
and by writing and performing poetry in Krio, Gladys also
promoted African culture at a time when many educated Africans
were inclined to disregard their true heritage.

Most worthy of respect and admiration, in my view, was the
enlightened consciousness that made her an outstanding example
of how best to live – with courage, humility, loving kindness and
good humour. She was always ready to offer help to people in
need. She always accentuated the positive in Africa, and

advocated unity among all Africans. In summary, Gladys Casely-Hayford was one of Africa's precious stones—an imperfect one, certainly, but nevertheless, a gem.

---OOOIIIOOO---

J.E. Casely-Hayford as a young man.

Gladys as a teenager.

Gladys as a young woman.

Adelaide Casely-Hayford in her early fifties.

J.E. Casely-Hayford in later life.

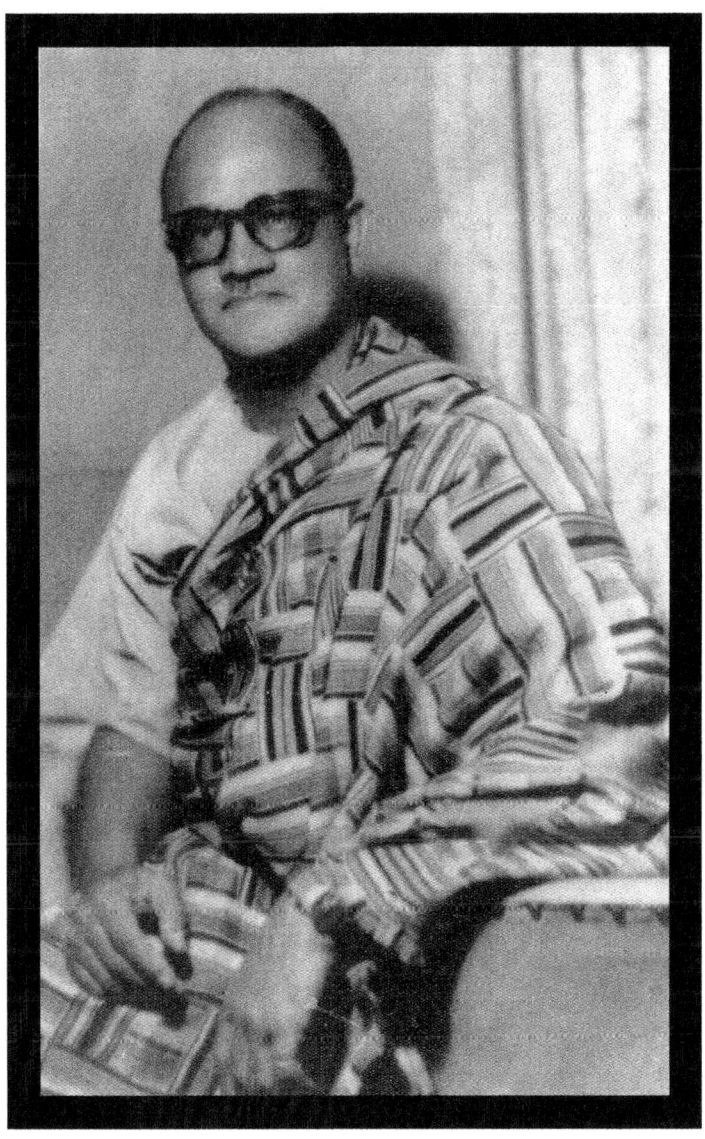

Gladys's brother, Archie Casely-Hayford in his prime.

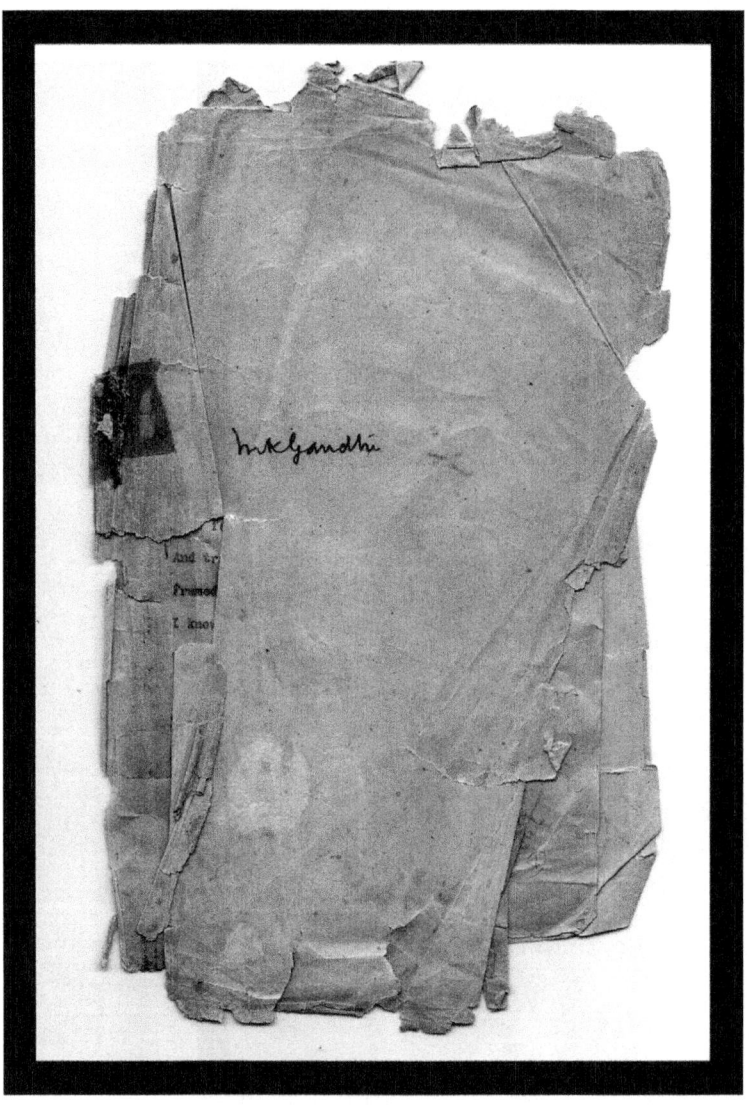

Gandhi's autograph still legible in Glady's collection of poems*

Arthur Hunter, Gladys's husband.

Gladys with small clay model of an African's head.

Gladys at the piano with Ralph Wright playing sax.
Her last performance in Freetown.

REFERENCES

1. Casely-Hayford, Adelaide and Casely-Hayford, Gladys. Mother and daughter: *Memoirs and poems*, edited by Lucilda Hunter. Freetown, The Sierra Leone University Press, 1983.
2. Cromwell, Adelaide M. *An African Victorian Feminist: the life and times of Adelaide Smith Casely Hayford 1868-1960.* Washington, D.C. Howard University Press, 1992 (First published, 1986).
3. Graves, Anna Melissa, editor. *Benvenuto Cellini had no prejudice against bronze. Letters from West Africans.* Baltimore, Waverly Press, 1943.

NOTES

Introduction
1. Sierra Leone Daily Mail., September 23, 1950.
2. Lewis, Roy. Sierra Leone: a modern portrait. London, Her Majesty's Stationery Office, 1954.
3. e.g. a) Anthology of Modern American Poetry, edited by Cary Nelson. Oxford University Press, 1999. b) Roses, Lorraine E. Harlem's Glory: black women writing 1900-1950. Harvard University Press, 1996.
4. Hayford, Joseph Ephraim Casely. Ethiopia unbound. London, C.M.Philips, 1911.

General note
Since so much of my information for the biography was obtained from Adelaide Casely-Hayford's *Memoirs* and her *Profile of Gladys,* specific annotations regarding material taken from these writings were made only when I considered it necessary.

Chapter One
1. The Creoles are the descendants of various settler communities in Freetown and its environs. The first groups of settlers were freed slaves and families who arrived from England in the 1780s and from Nova Scotia in 1792. They were followed by the Maroons who came from Jamaica in 1800 after successfully resisting slavery. Diverse groups of Africans liberated from slave ships joined the earlier settlers after 1807, as well as immigrants from the West Indies and elsewhere who came to serve the colonial government in various capacities and stayed on.
2. Langston Hughes. *An African Treasury. Articles, essays, stories, poems by Black Africans.* New York, Crown, 1960.

3. The Royal African Company was licensed by the English Crown to trade in West Africa.

4. *Memoirs*. Chapter Seven, p. 24-25.

5. Op.cit. p.25.

6. Encyclopedia of World Biography, edited by P. Byers. Detroit, Gale, 1998-

7. *An African Victorian Feminist,* Chapter VI p.64.

8. *Memoirs*. Chapter Seven. p.25.

9. *An African Victorian Feminist*. Chapter IX p.143.

10. *Memoirs*. Chapter Sixteen, p.58.

11. Information provided by Mr. Nokoe, unofficial historian of Axim.

12. Letter from Adelaide Casely-Hayford to her husband, February 7 1907. *An African Victorian Feminist*, Chapter VI, p.81

13. Op.cit. Letter from Adelaide Casely-Hayford to her husband dated October 5, 1906. Chapter VI, p.79.

14. Ibid. Letter from Adelaide Casely-Hayford to her husband, dated October 5, 1906. Chapter VI, p. 80.

15. Ibid. Letter from Adelaide Casely-Hayford to her husband, dated February 7, 1907. Chapter VI, p. 82.

16. *Memoirs*. Chapter Eight, p.28.

17. Op.cit. Chapter Eight, p.28.

18. Ibid. Chapter Nine, p.29.

19. Author's notes. *An African Victorian Feminist*. p.224.

20. *Memoirs*. Chapter Nine, p.31.

21. .*Profile Of Gladys*. In: *Memoirs and Poems*, p. 65-66.

22. Established in 1849, partly through a memorial fund set up by Anglican missionaries, Rev. and Mrs. Walsh, after the early death by accident of their daughter, Annie. The Annie Walsh Memorial School is the oldest secondary school for girls in Sierra Leone, if not West Africa.

23. Gladys was registered as pupil number 1405. Source: *The Annie Walsh Memorial School Register 1849-1999*, ed. Lulu Wright and Gladys Okoro-Cole. [Freetown, 2007].
24. Letter from Adelaide Casely-Hayford to J.E.Casely-Hayford, December 1918. *An African Victorian Feminist*. Chapter VII, p.94.
25. *Memoirs*. Chapter Nine, p.32.
26. Op.cit.----------------------------
27. From another version of Mrs. Casely-Hayford's memoirs. *An African Victorian Feminist*. Chapter VII, p.93.
28. Op. cit. Letter from Adelaide Casely-Hayford to J.E.Casely Hayford , December, 1918. Chapter VII, p.94.
29. Ibid. p.95.
30. Ibid. Letter from Adelaide Casely-Hayford to J.E. Casely Hayford dated January 19, 1920. p. 95

Chapter Two

1. *Profile of Gladys. Memoirs and Poems*, p.66.
2. Letter from Adelaide Casely-Hayford to J.E.Casely Hayford dated December 17, 1920. *An African Victorian Feminist*, Chapter VIII, p.123.
3. Op.cit. Letter from Adelaide Casely-Hayford to J.E.Casely Hayford, dated August 9, 1921. p.127.
4. Born 1875. Composer of the musical drama, 'Hiawatha' among other works. Except for visits to the United States, he lived his entire life in Britain and died there from pneumonia in 1912.
5. *Sierra Leone Weekly News*, August 20,1924. Cited in: An *African Victorian Feminist* Chapter VIII, p.119.
6. *Memoirs*. Chapter Eleven, p.35.
7. Gadzekpo, Audrey. The hidden history of gender in Ghanaian print cultures. Unpublished paper .[2002?]
8. James Emman Kwegyir Aggrey, born 1875 in Anomabu, British Gold Coast, died in America on July, 30 1927. A

famous West African educator and former vice-principal of Achimota School.

9. *Memoirs.* Chapter Fourteen, p.46.

Chapter Three

1. Letter from Beth Torrey to Anna Graves dated April 8 1932. *Benvenuto Cellini had no prejudice against bronze.* p.58.
2. *An African Victorian Feminist.* Notes on Chapter IX, p.221. Gladys's poems appeared in the Atlantic Monthly Vol. CXXXIX, January–June 1927, pp.489-490. They were accompanied by the following introduction: 'Aquah Laluah is a young African who studied for several years in Europe. She is a member of an ancient African family and the granddaughter of a native king'.
3. *Nativity* was originally entitled *Black Nativity.*
4. Gladys's original line 3 of *The Souls of Black and White* was: 'God laughed o'er one and left it white'.
5. *Opportunity, a Journal of Negro life,* New York, National Urban League 1923-1948. No.8, 1930.
6. *An African Victorian Feminist.* Chapter IX, p.148.
7. Op.cit. Notes on Chapter IX, p.224.

Chapter Four

1. Description of Gladys in a letter from Adelaide Casely-Hayford to Anna Graves dated June 27, 1931. *Benvenuto Cellini had no prejudice against bronze.* p. 41.
2. Op. cit. Editor's notes. p. 109.
3. Ibid. Letter from Gladys Casely-Hayford to Anna Graves dated July 10, 1931. p.91.
4. Letter from Adelaide Casely-Hayford to J.E.Casely-Hayford dated August 9, 1921. *An African Victorian Feminist.* Chapter VIII, p.127.

5. Letter from Adelaide Casely-Hayford to Anna Graves dated August 7, 1931. *Benvenuto Cellini had no prejudice against bronze.* p.49.
6. Op.cit. Editor's notes. p.101.
7. Ibid. Letter from Beth Torrey to Anna Graves.Ibid. p.59; and letter from Charles Easmon to Anna Graves dated April 23,1932. p. 64.
8. Ibid. Editor's notes. p.34.
9. Ibid. Letter from Charles Easmon to Anna Graves dated April 23, 1932. p.64.
10. Wright, Logie, editor. "Shine like de mornin' star". N.G.J. Ballanta of Sierra Leone, composer and ethnomusicologist. Undated pamphlet prepared by USAID for Ballanta Academy.
11. Nicholas Ballanta was born in Kissy Village, one of those established for liberated Africans in the 19th century. Kissy Village is located a few miles to the east of Freetown.
12. Letter from Beth Torrey to Anna Graves dated March 5, 1932. *Benvenuto Cellini had no prejudice against bronze*, pp. 57-8.
13. Op.cit Editor's notes. p.58.
14. Ibid. Editor's notes. p.58. Since my informant on Gladys's romance with Ballanta told me that he married an uneducated Liberian woman, I think Anna Graves confused one suitor with another, as it seems too much of a coincidence that two of Glady's suitors married uneducated Liberian women.
15. Ibid. Letter from Adelaide Casely-Hayford to Anna Graves dated April 21, 1932 p.60.
16. Ibid. Editor's notes. p.102.
17. *Memoirs.* Chapter Sixteen, p.58. Mrs. Casely-Hayford went on to say that this was generally true of very short people who, like Napoleon Bonaparte, tried to make up in self-assertion for the inches they lacked in stature.
18. Editor's notes. *Benvenuto Cellini had no prejudice against bronze.* p.46.

19. *Profile Of Gladys. Memoirs and Poems*, p.68.
20. Letter from Adelaide Casely-Hayford to Anna Graves dated June 27 1931.*Benvenuto had no prejudice against bronze.* p.41.

Chapter Five

1. Editor's notes. *Benvenuto Cellini had no prejudice against bronze,* p.34/5.
2. Op.cit. Letter from Gladys Casely-Hayford to Anna Graves dated July 15, 1931. p.94.
3. Ibid.
4. Ibid.
5. Ibid. Letter from Gladys Casely-Hayford to Anna Graves dated July 21, 1931. p.96.
6. Ibid.
7. Ibid.
8. Ibid. Letter from Adelaide Casely-Hayford to Anna Graves dated July 11, 1931 p.43.
9. Ibid.
10. Ibid. Letter from Gladys Casely-Hayford to Anna Graves dated July 15, 1931. p.94/95.
11. Ibid. Letter from Adelaide Casely-Hayford to Anna Graves dated October 12, 1931. p.52.
12. Ibid. Letter from Adelaide Casely-Hayford to Anna Graves dated July 11, 1931. p.43.
13. Ibid. Letter from Adelaide Casely-Hayford to Anna Graves dated May 29, 1931. p.39
14. Ibid. Letter from Beth Torrey to Anna Graves, dated April 8, 1932 p.58.
15. Ibid. Letter from Gladys Casely-Hayford to Anna Graves dated August 28, 1931. p.100.
16. Ibid.
17. Ibid. Letter from Adelaide Casely-Hayford to Anna Graves dated June,_27, 1931.p.41.

18. Ibid. Letter from Adelaide Casely-Hayford to Anna Graves dated October 12, 1931. p.52.
19. Ibid. Letter from Adelaide Casely-Hayford to Anna Graves dated July 24, 1931. p.46.
20. Ibid. Letter from Gladys Casely-Hayford to Anna Graves dated May 19, 1931. p.88.
21. Ibid. Editor's notes. p.101.
22. Ibid. Letter from Adelaide Casely-Hayford to Anna Graves dated July 24, 1931. p.46.
23. Ibid. Letter from Gladys Casely-Hayford to Anna Graves dated July 6 1931. p.89/90.
24. Ibid. Editor's notes. p.102.
25. Founded in 1899, Ruskin College is an independent educational institution located in Oxford, but not part of the University. It provides educational opportunities for adults with few or no qualifications. (Source: Wikipedia, the free online encyclopedia).
26. Editor's notes. *Benvenuto Cellini had no prejudice against bronze*. p.102.

Chapter Six

1. Letter from Gladys Casely-Hayford to Anna Graves dated July 10, 1931. *Benvenuto Cellini had no prejudice against bronze*, p.91.
2. Op.cit. Letter from Gladys Casely-Hayford to Anna Graves dated July 14, 1931. p.92.
3. Ibid. Letter from Gladys Casely-Hayford to Anna Graves dated July 15, 1931. p.93.
4. Ibid. Letter from Gladys Casely-Hayford to Anna Graves dated July 21, 1931. p.97.
5. Ibid. Letter from Adelaide Casely-Hayford to Anna Graves dated July 11, 1931. p.42.
6. Ibid. Letter from Gladys Casely-Hayford to Anna Graves dated July 27, 1931. p.98.

7. Ibid.
8. Ibid. Letter from Gladys Casely-Hayford to Anna Graves dated August 28, 1931. p.101.
9. Ibid. Editor's notes. p.104.
10. Ibid. Letter from Gladys Casely-Hayford to Anna Graves dated September 8, 1931. p.105.
11. Ibid. Letter from Gladys Casely-Hayford to Anna Graves dated September 15, 1931. p.105.
12. Ibid. Letter from Gladys Casely-Hayford to Anna Graves dated October 14, 1931. p.106.
13. Ibid. Letter from Adelaide Casely-Hayford to Anna Graves dated August 22, 1931. p.51.
14. Ibid. Letter from Adelaide Casely-Hayford to Anna Graves dated October 12, 1931. p.52.
15. Ibid. Letter from Gladys Casely-Hayford to Anna Graves dated October 14, 1931. p.106.
16. Ibid.
17. Ibid. Letter from Gladys Casely-Hayford to Anna Graves dated November 25, 1931. p.107.
18. Ibid. Letter from Adelaide Casely-Hayford to Anna Graves dated December 5, 1931. p.53.
19. Ibid. Letter from A. Barratt Brown to Anna Graves dated December 18, 1931. p.54.
20. Ibid. Letter from A. Barratt Brown to Anna Graves dated February 29 1932. p.54.
21. Ibid. Letter from Gladys Casely-Hayford to Anna Graves dated July 21, 1932. p.96. Archie Casely-Hayford's daughter, Désirée Sheldrake assured me that he loved Gladys dearly but did not understand the artistic temperament. His lack of financial support while Gladys was in Europe might therefore have been an attempt to discourage her from continuing her bohemian lifestyle.
22. *Profile of Gladys. Memoirs and Poems*, p.66.

Chapter Seven

1. Editor's notes. *Benvenuto Cellini had no prejudice against bronze*, p. 105.
2. Op.cit.Letter from Adelaide Casely-Hayford to Anna Graves dated March 22, 1932. p.56.
3. Ibid. Letter from A. Barratt Brown to Anna Graves dated March 9, 1932. p.55.
4. Ibid. Letter from Charles Easmon to Anna Graves dated April 23, 1932. p.63.
5. Ibid. Letter from Charles Easmon to Anna Graves dated May 5, 1932. p.64.
6. Ibid. Editor's notes. p.65.
7. Ibid. Letter from Charles Easmon to Anna Graves dated May 31, 1932. p.66.
8. Ibid. Editor's notes. p.67.
9. Ibid. Editor's notes. p.66.
10. Ibid. Letter from A Barratt Brown to Anna Graves dated June 13, 1932. p.68.
11. Ibid. Letter from A Barratt Brown to Anna Graves dated June 23, 1932. p.68.
12. Ibid. Letters from Adelaide Casely-Hayford to Anna Graves dated May, 4, 1932 and May 17 1932. pp. 60-62.
13. Ibid.
14. Ibid. Letter from Adelaide Casely-Hayford to Anna Graves dated June 1, 1932. p.67.
15. Ibid. Editor's notes. p.67.
16. Ibid. Letter from Adelaide Casely-Hayford to Anna Graves dated July 6, 1932. p.69.
17. Ibid.
18. Ibid. Letter from Adelaide Casely-Hayford to Anna Graves dated July 28, 1932. p.71.
19. Ibid.
20. Ibid.

21. Ibid. Letter from Adelaide Casely-Hayford to Anna Graves dated November 16, 1932. pp.73-74.
22. Jamison, Kay Redfield. *Touched with fire: manic depressive illness and the artistic temperament.* New York, The Free Press, 1993.
23. Letter from Adelaide Casely-Hayford to Anna Graves dated January 10, 1942. *Benvenuto Cellini had no prejudice against bronze.* p.86.

Chapter Eight

1. Letter from Gladys Casely-Hayford to Anna Graves dated November 16, 1932. *Benvenuto Cellini had no prejudice against bronze.* p 107.
2. Op.cit.Letter from Adelaide Casely-Hayford to Anna Graves dated November 16, 1932. p.73.
3. Ibid. p.74
4. Ibid. Letter from Adelaide Casely-Hayford to Anna Graves dated August 8, 1933. p.75.
5. Ibid. Letter from Adelaide Casely-Hayford to Anna Graves dated August 23, 1934. p. 79.
6. Ibid. Letter from Gladys Casely-Hayford to Anna Graves dated July 5, 1934. p. 108. Gladys probably considered all her non-English poems as being written in Broken English(pidgin) ; but there is a noticeable difference between *Take Um So*, below, which contains more pure English words and phrases, and others included in the selection in Annex 2. It seems that Gladys's Krio, the language spoken by Creoles, improved as time went on. Krio is no longer considered 'broken English' since it has a distinct grammatical structure and a vocabulary with many non-English words. Gladys was one of the pioneers of Krio literature.

Take Um So

Na den take um so bobo kin better
Na den take um so titi kin wise,

En den take am so daddy, en den take um so mammy
Kin eat den fat fowl bone, en win de prize.

If God gie you abulay or bamboo 'ouse or pan,
Or den stone an' cement mansion whey some get.
If God gie you life of leisure en concur all you plan,
Or E turn en gie you worry , no for fret, take um so.

If God full some 'ouse wid piken en E nor gree full you yone,
Or E gie you don E take de piken back,
Or E show you road way tranga en E put you for climb hill,
En guide some oder person pan broad track…take um so.

If water full you yeye from morning so tay night,
En discouragement so mona you, you no get strength for
fegt,
No fraid…de one whey gie you Eenself go set you right,
Take um so.

Because you nor get sense for see the working of
Nor forget say "The Eternal is most wonderfully kind".
God en guidance dey before you God en mercy dey behind,
Take um so.

7. Cited in An African Victorian Feminist, Chapter X, p.160.
8. Arthur Hunter died in 1972, aged 60 which made his date of birth 1912.
9. Information provided by Kobina Hunter.
10. Arthur Hunter told me this himself and showed me the scars which were still visible.
11. Letter from Adelaide Casely-Hayford to Anna Graves dated April 29, 1936. *Benvenuto Cellini had no prejudice against bronze,* p.80.

12. Op.cit. Letter from Adelaide Casely-Hayford to Anna Graves dated November 23, 1936. p.82.
13. Ibid. Letter from Gladys Casely-Hayford to Anna Graves dated September 20, 1936. p. 108.
14. Quoted in *An African Victorian feminist*, Chapter X, p.158.
15. Letter from Adelaide Casely-Hayford to Anna Graves dated January 10, 1942. *Benvenuto Cellini had no prejudice against bronze.* p.86.
16. Désirée Sheldrake, her mother, Essie Casely-Hayford, and her brothers, Beattie and Louis, were rescued and put ashore in Freetown after their ship was torpedoed by the Germans during the Second World War. They spent a year with the Freetown Casely-Hayfords. Désirée remembers that her mother and Gladys started a café for soldiers. It is therefore possible that the failure of the café was partly due to Désirée's return to the Gold Coast.
17. Op. cit. p.86.
18. Ibid. Letter from Adelaide Casely-Hayford to Anna Graves dated November 7, 1942. p.87.
19. *An African Victorian Feminist.* Chapter X, p.160
20. Désirée Sheldrake is sure Gladys must have spent most of her time in Accra with her brother and his first wife as she and her sister-in-law, Essie Casely-Hayford, got along splendidly. They shared a passionate interest in the arts.

Chapter Nine
1. The Wilberforce Memorial Hall burned down in 1959.
2. One of Dr. Cromwell's informants mentioned that the Tuboku-Metzger brothers, Constance and Sam, helped Gladys with painting backdrops. *An African Victorian Feminist.* p.189.
3. Op.cit. 189.
4. Ibid. Notes on Chapter X, p.224.

5. *Take Um So*. Freetown, New Era Press, 1948. Despite the best efforts of myself and librarian friends, the only copy of this publication tracked down was in London, England, in the St. Pancras Reading Room of the British Library. We were, however, unable to retrieve it later, due to the library's copyright regulations.

6. *Profile of Gladys. Memoirs and Poems*. p.67.

7. Op.cit. p.68.

8. Ibid. pp.66-7.

9. Letter from Adelaide Casely-Hayford to Anna Graves dated August 23. 1934. *Benevenuto Cellini had no prejudice against bronze* p .79.

10. Op.cit. Letter from Adelaide Casely-Hayford to Anna Graves dated May 17, 1932. p. 62.

11.Editor's notes in p.103.

Annex One

The Magic Calabash

Listen children, to a story of the magic calabashes or 'Take
me, take me, take me."

ONCE, in a little African town, whose streets ran crazily like red
ribbons over Mother Earth, and which was green with the
verdure of tropical plants and flowers, there lived a woman
named Mammy Camacama. She had a very beautiful daughter
called Ayo. Slender of form was she, smooth of skin; and her hair
of the hue of night, hid in it all the sunbeams shed from the year's
beginning to its end. Her hands, black and beautifully shaped,
with palms like warm tea roses, were absolutely untrained for
useful tasks:

Ayo's Song:

I don't know how to make a fire,
I don't know how to cook,
I don't know how to beat the rice,
Or wash clothes in the brook.
But I can dance, dance, dance so spritely,
Every body knows;
And I twirl, twirl so lightly,
Twirl upon my toes,
Twirl upon my toes.

It was Remi, her little step-sister, whose hands could rock a
cradle, soothe a sick person, concoct the rarest African delicacies
and weave the loveliest patterns. Hers were the loveliest beaded
bodices and aprons in this town:

Remi's song:

I do know how to make a fire,
I do know how to cook,
I do know how to beat the rice.
And wash clothes in the brook.
But I'm much too tired for dancing,
Everybody knows;
And I work until I'm aching
From my head to my toes,
Aching from my head to my toes.

Though Ayo's mouth was fashioned beautifully, it was Remi that had the sweetest curves. Though Ayo's beauty shone upon all like the brilliant tropical moon that lights up the deep blue of the sky at night, it was Remi's sunny expression that warmed the heart. Though Ayo was clothed in the richest garments money could buy, it was Remi whose dignity of bearing was that of a princess who had inadvertently left her throne to live among beggars.

The Sisters' Song:

We are two sisters though no one could ever tell,
And no matter what befalls us,
We will love each other well,
We will love each other well.

Mammy Camacama was blind to Remi's lovable nature and her charming disposition. The only point that she ever remembered was that Remi was her step-daughter. She was therefore to be hated because, through her, Mammy Camacama was reminded that her husband had once loved another, perhaps even better than she herself had been loved; although during his lifetime he had showered her with every possible gift supposed to bring happiness. Now that he was dead, her smouldering jealousy of this child was allowed to kindle into a flame that fed itself on petty, unkind actions all day. It kept her from sleeping at night, planning some new means of spite, some cruel word that would sting, some hint that would drop poison into Remi's cup of happiness for the day.

This was the situation when Remi was sent to the waterside one beautiful morning to get water with Mammy Camacama's best calabash, with the injunction to be quick about it, and refrain from idleness on the penalty of a sound beating.

Remi stepped lightly down the path. It was always a pleasure to her to get water, because of the beauty of the stream. Its loveliness was indescribable, full of a deep soul-stirring beauty and quiet loveliness. This day the current was dangerous, owing to its having rained previously, and it happened that the calabash slipped out of her hands and careered merrily down the stream, bobbing up and down on the surface of the water. Remi plunged in after it, but had to return owing to the terrifying current. She then ran, dripping wet, along the bank to try and retrieve it, but the calabash had disappeared completely.

"What!" cried Mammy Camacama, "you have returned without that calabash? Go and find it, and do not dare to let me see even your shadow darken this doorstep unless you bring it with you."

Remi wandered back to the banks of the stream and sobbed herself to sleep after singing:

Alas, oh dear, woe is me,
I can't go home tonight.
I've lost my mother's calabash
And she's driven me away.
Oh moon, look down
And shed your kindly light

On this poor wandering child
Who has no home tonight.
O God, look down,
And me from danger keep
Watch o'er a little child
As she falls asleep.

The next day, she resolved to dive to the bottom again and see whether she could recover some particle of the calabash which she supposed must have been dashed to pieces on the jagged stones. The water was so cool to her fevered body, so cool, that deep down she sank, down – down – and to her amazement, instead of touching the bed of the stream, she landed in a little lane that led up to a thatched hut. After gazing about her for a long time and seeing no sign of life, she timidly walked to the door of the hut and knocked. From within she heard the following song:

"Because I am a witch, a witch, a witch,
Because I am a witch, a witch;
I can kill, I can slay,
I can turn night into day."

So long as I do nothing to harm her, thought Remi, she cannot possibly harm me, even if she is the wickedest witch in the world, so she knocked gently on the door again and said, "Good morning, Ma."

"Who is that?" called out the witch in shrill tones, "My name is Remi, Ma. I have come to look for my calabash, Ma."

The old witch rose from her low stool and came forward. She looked very much like an old grandmother, but her face was evil.

'You are not afraid of me?' Leaning on her stick, the witch shot out this question and closed her ugly mouth tight.

'No,' answered Remi, quite truthfully, for there was no evil in her; and she smiled shyly.

'Well, do you see that sieve? Go and get me some water in it."

'Yes, Ma' said Remi obediently.

After wandering a few yards away, she came to a tiny stream, and though she had felt a little nervous at the thought of trying to fill a sieve with water, she was amazed to find that such a feat was possible. Singing softly to herself, she came back.

'Please, Ma, I have brought your water.'

'You see those stones there?' The witch then pointed with a gnarled forefinger to the tiny pebbles strewed before her doorway.

'Put some in the mortar and pound them for me. I am hungry."

'Yes, Ma,' said the ever obedient Remi. Her deft fingers found it an easy task to collect enough stones for a meal. Then she walked over to the mortar and poured them in. Taking up the wooden pestle, she began to beat the pebbles. Perspiration flowed down her body; for beating stones is no easy task and requires a lot of physical energy. Slowly, under her methodical, rhythmic strokes, the pebbles began to soften. Gradually they broke up and began to assume the tiny, long pellet shape of African rice grains.

Panting for breath, Remi went back to the witch where she sat brooding, her fierce old eyes peering greedily about her, her long, thin fingers clutching and unclutching her stick.

'Go take that pot, make a fire and boil the rice,' commanded the witch.

'Yes, Ma,' said Remi and went to the corner of the room where stood three stones in readiness for cooking. In vain Remi searched the whole room and the tiny yard for wood. Not a twig was to be seen. She wondered how she was going to boil the rice without a fire, but remembering the miracles already accomplished, she went back to the corner, placed the rice, after washing it, in the pot with enough water to cover it, and waited for it to boil.

After what seemed like an incredibly long time, the steam began to thread its spiral way up to the thatched roof, then one little bubble appeared, then another, and the whole pot then boiled merrily. Remi watched it carefully, stirring it so it would not burn, adding more water when necessary. At last her patience was rewarded. She dished up the rice and took it to the witch, saying,

'I have finished, Ma.'

'My child, you have done well,' the witch grumbled grudgingly. 'Now, go to the garden over there. You will see a lot of calabashes growing. Some will say, 'Take me, take me', and some will say, 'Don't take me, don't take me. You should take one of the ones that say, 'Don't take me.'

'Yes, Ma,' said Remi and ran out into the yard, through a tiny gate, into the witch's garden. Along the wall, and spreading for miles and miles the calabash plants grew and from them, like the whispering of the wind, came the sound of their tiny voices, 'Take me, take me', and from the opposite wall, 'Don't take me, don't take me.'

Remi, remembering the witch's injunction, deliberately turned her back on those that said, 'Take me, take me' and plucked one of the others which sobbed out, 'Don't take me, don't take me,' and, tucking it under her arm, she retraced her footsteps.

'My child', said the witch, 'Goodbye. Go now.'

So Remi smiled up at her, radiant with joy, for if she could not give Mammy Camacama her old calabash, she could at least make atonement by offering her this new one. As she reached the end of the path, she found herself suddenly immersed in water, and very soon she had gained the surface. Then she struck out for shore again, swimming with a side stroke, so as not to lose the precious calabash.

By this time Mammy Camacama, who had been suffering from qualms of conscience, and black looks and insinuations from all her neighbours, was wishing from the bottom of her heart that Remi had not taken her at her word and disappeared for good. Imagine her relief therefore, when she saw Remi serenely coming down the winding road to the house. However, she suddenly stifled the remorse she was feeling and refused to open the door although she heard Remi singing,

"Open the door, stepmother,
Now I need no more roam;
I've brought you a new calabash
So please, Mother, open the door."

Mammy Camacama yelled out spitefully,

"Go away, go away, I do not believe you.
I know it is not true,
Go away, you dirty ruffian, go away.
I will not open to you."

It was Ayo who eventually opened the door.

"Oh, so you have come. You have brought the calabash," said Mammy Camacama, slightly mollified, and extremely annoyed that Remi had won as usual. 'Bring a knife, Ayo dear, let me open the calabash."

When the gourd was cut open, out came the most precious and beautiful things that money can buy, besides gold coins and jewels.

Mammy Camacama's jubilant song when she see the riches
When we move, when we move, when we move into our new house,
There'll be boys to help and maids to serve,
When we move into our new house

With these new possessions, the whole family was now able to move into a new house and to join the upper strata of society which they were able to enter because of their amazing wealth. Remi, who was instrumental in bringing about this change of fortune was the least benefited, yet daily she grew more beautiful.

Money does not last forever, and when the small fortune dwindled to a sum of two figures, Mammy Camacama, now styled 'Madam', began to cast about in her mind for fresh supplies. She called Ayo privately; bade her put on her oldest clothes, go down to the stream, let an old calabash float down it, and then go to the witch for a new one. Ayo, with deep grumbling, went. On reaching the stream, she shoved the calabash viciously into the water, watched it bob merrily downstream, and then plunged into the water after it. Not having learnt to swim, she flopped into the path below in a most undignified fashion, and swore as she picked herself up.

What a funny looking place this is, she thought to herself. Then she walked insolently up to the door of the witch's home, and unceremoniously poked her head into the doorway. The old witch was just that moment crooning to herself:

"Because I am a witch, a witch, a witch,
Because I am a witch, a witch,
I can kill, I can slay,
I can turn night into day."

Ayo's heart gave a violent thump as she heard this and she laughed nervously. The witch swung around.

'Who are you, you rude child?' she asked.

'I am not your child, and I am not rude,' returned Ayo. 'And as to who I am, that is none of your business; where is my calabash?'

'All in good time, child, all in good time,' she replied, 'Take that sieve over there and get me some water.'

'What do you think I am, a fool? How can a sieve hold water?'

'Do as you are told!' ordered the witch sharply.

Ayo, shuddering with fright, picked up the sieve, and tiptoed into the yard. She eventually found the stream and filled the sieve, having to go backwards and forward a great many times because she kept spilling the water.

'Here is your water, and now where is my calabash?'

'All in good time,' the witch repeated. 'Take those stones and beat me some rice out of them.'

'Do you think I am a fool?' Ayo shrieked again, almost choking with rage. 'How can stones turn into rice? If I did not want my calabash, I would not obey you.'

And because she did not approach the task in the right spirit, she found it very difficult; her hands were bruised and torn before she finished, and tears of anger and fatigue stood in her eyes. At last she finished the beating.

'Now,' commanded the witch, 'put it in that pot over there and boil it.'

'What! boil without a fire? What do you think I am? How will it get cooked?'

'You just do as you are told,' snapped the witch.

Ayo was obliged to set to. She burnt the rice and got the steam into her face. When she finished, she flung the rice at the old woman's feet, saying,

'Here is your rice. Now where is my calabash?'

'Well, child, go to the garden over there. You will find some calabashes. Some will say, 'Take me, take me,'and others, 'Don't take me, Don't take me.' Take one of those that say, 'Don't take me.'

Ayo flounced proudly out of the hut, resolving to do exactly as she pleased in the matter. She found the calabashes without difficulty and doggedly took one of those that said, 'Take me, take me.' She then floated to the surface, swallowing a lot of water as she made her way through. At last she managed to get ashore and then ran home. Her mother made the pretence of not wanting to open the door, and it was Remi who opened the door for her.

When they opened the calabash, toads, frogs, lizards, snakes and every conceivable thing that is evil tumbled out of it. Mammy Camacama and her daughter, Ayo, fled, pursued by these creatures.

Mammy Camacama and Ayo's song as they flee:

Fly away, fly away,
Destruction comes on us today.
Snakes and toads, lizards, frogs,
Spirits, moles, cats and dogs.
Fly away, fly away, fly......y.

Thus is the story ended.

*Though this is the narrative version, of *The Magic Calabash*, I have inserted original songs from the musical play in appropriate places. Apart from the witch's song, the words were obtained by listening to a recording of *The Magic Calabash* made by my mother some years before she passed away. I have been reminded that in the musical play of the Magic Calabash, the names of the two girls were Tunde and Ayo.

Annex Two

Additional poems & songs
by Gladys Casely-Hayford

THESE poems are a personal selection from the more than three hundred and fifty Gladys wrote. I have not included poems already in the main body of the biography or in the notes relating to specific chapters, but the reader is referred to the chapters where they can be found. I took the liberty of giving titles to untitled poems wherever I could. They are indicated with an asterisk (*). Also, in order to make the poems more appealing to the modern reader, I replaced one or two archaic words and spellings where doing so did not interfere with the rhythm or sense of the verse.

Poems Inspired by Africa, Africans
& the Black Experience

A Marvellous Thing*

Let my singing burst on a major note
Check the minor lilt in the Negro's throat.

But how can the Negroes play their harps,
With sorrow for intervals, pain for sharps?

Though the tempo is kept by the gleaming stars,
Notation is writ on prejudice bars.

With a knife in the wound, and tears on the face,
Should the song be quavers in the treble or bass?

If God gives no sign when we end the refrain,

Have we the courage to start again?

With conflicting fugues and odd time to keep,
It's a wonder we laugh, as well as weep.

To me it is a marvellous thing
That in spite of it all, the Negro can sing!

April 20th, 1929.

Africa's Need

We need pure women, pure of soul and mind;
Purity is the power of humankind.
We need pure men, men pure enough to hold
A woman's honour, of more wealth than gold,
And children born in light, not in disgrace.
More purity, fresh purity, O race,
Then shall our lips be cleansed to hymn each height,
"On, forward, upward, Africa march on:
Our manhood virile, and our women pure,
Shackles unbound, to leap through Freedom's door.
March on through wrong into your heritage and your soul's right.
March on, inheritors of Afric's might. March on!"

African Schoolgirls' Song

Beat, beat, beat, dears, beat the golden grain,
For food builds up the sinews, and stimulates the
Just as you beat rice, dears, with your pestle in your
You'll beat distrust and bloodshed out of Africa our

Clean, clean, clean, dears, clean the silver fish.
Drop its shimmering, shining scales, then lay it on the dish;
'Tis destined in the future, little Africans, that you
Shall clean the scales that hide true Africa from view.
Burn, burn, burn, dears, burn the sweet palm oil,
And every mother's son, dears, will thank you for the toil.
For in the years to come, dears, while other nations shout,
You'll burn the heart of Africa, till all its dross burns out.

Grind, grind, grind, dears, pepper ripe and red,
For there are many hungry, eager, strong, black lads, who must be
fed;
Your dear black hands that guide the stone will remain faithful
still,
To guide and comfort Africa, when passing through life's mill.

Beat for Me, Sangbye

Beat for me, Sangbye, beat,
A devil is in my heart;
My heart is a burden of heavy pain
And my eyes are twin pools of falling rain.
Beat for me, Sangbye, beat.

Beat for me, Sangbye, beat
Till desire leaps in the blood
Till it blots out my despair and ire
And ignites the spark of some other fire,
Beat for me Sangbye beat.

Beat for me, Sangbye, beat,
Coquettry for her charms.
Pulsing rhythm for rhythmic feet

And love for her empty arms;
Beat for her, Sangbye, beat.

Beat till her head bends back
Revealing her dusky throat,
Beat till her full breasts rise
Like a single rounded note.
Beat till her bosom heaves
With the heavy perfume of her breath.
Beat till emotion surges so deep
That she sways to the brink of death.
Till she knows that in her swooning
Strong arms will hold her up;
Beat till she knows that bruising lips
Will fill her passion's cup.
Beat till she knows her throbbing breasts
Will by trembling hands be cupped.
Beat till she knows that the feast of love
Once laid is always supped.

Beat for me, Sangbye, beat.
Slowly I now draw near
Trembling from longing and deep desire
Shaken by doubt and fear.

I touch her and on we sway,
A light leaps out of her eyes,
I caress her hair and her heart throbs grow
As faint as a soul that dies.
Beat for me, Sangbye, beat,
In delirium let me forget.
Her shoulders are falling against my breast,
But she is not conquered yet.

I touch her neck with my lips,
In a circle the dancers sway.
I draw her closer and kiss her eyes,
And lead her gently away.

With the crescent moon above,
Damp grasses beneath my feet,
I draw her unto my bosom,
Beat for me, Sangbye, beat.

She lies in my strong arms sleeping,
And I draw an exhausted breath,
We have hovered upon the perilous bridge
Love spans, 'twixt life and death.

But when she awakens once more
To the clear warm morning skies,
Will love draw the heavy lids down again,
Or cold hate gleam from her eyes?

I know not, I trow not, I care not,
A devil is in my feet,
I am kin to the stalking leopard,
I dance too on padded feet.
I am desire seeking prey,
Beat for me, Sangbye, beat.

Tomorrow may come with regrets,
But who heeds tomorrow or fears
Today I will live to the uttermost,
And tomorrow bathe in my tears.
Beat for me, Sangbye, beat.

Black Folk

"Why do the bards of black folk
Sing grief brushed over with gladness?"
"Because God sculptured the soul of the race
In a moment of wistful sadness."

"Why do the bards of black folk
Sing of joy that follows all sorrow?"
"God's tool when he chiseled the soul of the race
was 'The-Hope-of-the-Unborn-Morrow' ".

Character Sketch

Dady is a crew man
With tribe marks on his face,
Flat-footed and bare-footed
He rolls about the place.
Because I said "Good morning", he couldn't do enough,
But offered me with gallantry,
A pinch of snuff.

"Do good, marm, clear the cold
Right way out of your head."
I hadn't got a cold at, all, but that's what Dady said.
Twixt gnarled thumb and forefinger, he proferred me the stuff,
And bowing low,
He drawled out slow,
"A pinch of snuff."

He found a file I'd lost,
I gave him one round shilling
'Cause he was old and worked so hard,
And was so downright willing.

Above all, we're both black, and that's bond enough,
Twas given free, through sympathy,
That pinch of snuff.

Rainy Season Love Song
(West African)

Out of the tense awed darkness my Frangipani comes,
Whilst the blades of Heaven flash round her and the roll of
thunder drums.
My young heart leaps and dances with exquisite joy and pain,
As storm within, and storm without, I meet my love in the rain.
"The rain is in love with you, darling; 'tis kissing you everywhere,
Rain pattering over you small brown feet, rain in your curly hair;
Rain in the vale that your twin breasts make, as in
delicate mounds they rise,
I hope there is rain in your heart, Frangipani, as rain
half fills your eyes."
Into my arms she cometh, and the lightning of my desire
Flashes and leaps about her, more subtle than Heaven's fire.
"The lightning's in love with you, darling, it is loving
you so much,
That its electricity pulses in you, wherever I may touch.
When I kiss your lips and your eyes, and your hands like twin
flowers apart,
I know there is lightning, Frangipani, deep in the depths of your
heart."
The thunder rumbles about us, and I feel its triumphant note,
As your warm arms steal about me, and I kiss your dusky throat.

"The thunder's in love with you, darling, it hides its
power in your breast,
And I feel it stealing over me, as I lie in your arms at

rest.

I sometimes wonder, beloved, when I drink from life's proferred bowl,

Whether there's thunder hidden in the innermost parts

The Harmattan

There's a buoyance in the weather, there's a swaying in the tree,
There's a whirring of bird's feather, there's the lightness of the breeze,
There's a radiance in the sunshine, and the atmosphere
Like the cutting of a cameo, for the Harmattan is here.
There's a brightness in the flowers, a soft whiteness in the moon;
There's a lilt to which the hours dance to the day's soft tune,
There's a softness in all nature, and a pathos in her tear,
As she palpitates and trembles, for the Harmattan is here.

It is here in leaping pulses, in the clear and vital brain,
Where free limbs and flowing movements, where lethargicness lies slain.
Born in new determination, in fresh vigour everywhere,
In the stirring of fresh impulse, for the Harmattan is here.

See it glows in the recesses of alert wide open eyes;
With fresh visions leading onward to new hopes of paradise.
It curves the red lips parted in sweet eloquence of speech,
It is born in springs restarted, in deep sources, out of reach

Where the Eternal Spirit, where the vital glowing wind
Sweeps purifying all the ranks of erring human kind.
Tis the breath of God that wakens and breathes blessings everywhere,
Tis His sweet keen pure revival when the Harmattan is here.

The Rainy Season

The Air is full of atmospheric pain,
Dark-faced, distorted, by its awful strain,
She bursts in paroxysms of wild rain,
And then exhausted, calms herself again.

Tom-toms

Beat, beat, beat tom-toms beat.
The leopard is a yellow streak of cunning and deceit;
The leopard is four-footed death, with silent padded feet;
Beat, beat, beat tom-toms beat.

Moan, moan, moan, tom-toms moan.
The jungle has a magic and a mystery all is own,
And the singing of the drums vibrates its fearful monotone;
Moan, moan,moan, tom-toms moan.

Shriek, shriek, shriek, tom-toms shriek.
The forest has a thousand tongues and let each tongue now speak;
The forest has a mighty voice, but the human voice is weak;
And lest it be lost and heard no more, shriek aloud, shriek tom-toms shriek.
Sing, sing, sing, tom-toms sing.
The bat and the night moths flitter; the air is a quivering thing
Where love palpitates and trembles and brushes the night jar's wing,
Sing, sing, sing, tom-toms sing.

Wail, wail, wail, tom-toms wail.
The fire of Heaven sweeps o'er us and only man is frail;

The sky is a flash of running fire and the sky is lightning pale;
But the spirits omnipotent circle the camp, their power
Wail, wail, wail, tom-toms wail.

Laugh, laugh, laugh tom-toms laugh.
Life is at best but a space before rest and the interim is chaff;
And contentment makes the heart lie still and cuts all sorrow in
half.
Laugh, laugh, laugh, tom-toms laugh.

Beat, beat, beat, tom-toms, beat.
Moan out your weird sad tones, quiver with laughter;
Shriek, wail and sing and laugh; why mind what comes after?

Toussaint L' Overture

With a stroke of his pen the great soldier Napoleon
Reduced islands to slaves.
"My councillors, what shall we do to Domingo over the waves?"
Answered slave holders, "Plantations suffer, since we've released
the Negro from chains.
Crops either rot or mature and lie wasted. Where are our gains?
Sweating from early dawn until sunset, with nought for our
pains."
"Boric, it seems Saint Domingo's protesting, for L'Overture's
secretary sends this to France,
"God raised up a man to govern yon island, give it a chance,
Plunge not its happiness and full prosperity back into war,
Saint Domingo's the happiest of all the dominions you've had
heretofore.
Culture is climbing the slopes of the mountains, there's trade in
its waters from over all seas.
Laughter and freedom sing in their fountains, health and
contentment blow in each breeze.

What would you more with a God-given ruler, over all these?"
Napoleon smiled at the end of the letter, "Boric, I wonder if all
this is true,
With Lerec as captain and you as commander, go take
Besides, with five thousand troops idle, some mischief must
brew."
Thus did France load her heavy war galleons, in eighteen hundred
with death in her hold,
Stark death in her cannons, her poops and her quarterdecks, trim
for the slaughter with hatreds of old.
Among them mulattos, L'Overture's enemies, a full fifty
thousand all told.
Holland sent sixty ships, England was neutral, Napoleon's
galleons were powerful and strong.
America, brimming with slaves, sent hostility, thus they came on.
L'Overture gazed at the advancing flotilla,
his horse cropped the grass as he loosened the rein,
"Shall we be mown down like grass in our meadows? Shall we be
slain?"
Back to the hills quickly galloped L'Toussaint, raised up his
standard and sent forth his cry:
"God gave us liberty, God gave us freedom. Fighting we die.
Burn down the cities, destroy the harvests, tear up the
Fight over the ashes, beat back the invaders, show the white man,
when he comes, his own hell.
Fighting to death we retain our old liberty, go down untrammeled
into our graves.
God gave us freedom, God gave us liberty. Shall we be slaves?
Cannon and rifle shot thundering, hurl them back to
the waves."
Lerec sent word to Christopher saying he and his army
Immediate fires leapt from each store house and steeple at
Toussaint's command.
Sword hilt to hilt, shout for shout intermingling, they

fought hand to hand,
Sprinkling warm embers and ashes with bloodshed strewing the sand.
Cannon and bayonet, rifle and shell, thunder and blood and hell, still Toussaint's cry:
"God gave us liberty, God gave us freedom. Fighting we die."
Advancing, retreating, L'Overture beating, till none could distinguish blood stains from red coats.
"Men run for your lives, we are beaten," cried Lerec, "back to the boats!"
"Keep on, my children, "L'Overture urged them; his troops staggered wounded, eyes blood blurred
When there rose like a sob from the ranks of the Negroes, the Marseillaise hymn.
Whispered white officers, "Lerec you hear it? How can we give the command to advance?
How can we rally against old traditions? Can we fight France?"
"Hold on you cowards," yelled Lerec, their leader,
"Open fresh fusillades! Charge! Rush! Attack!"
But his soldiers, still thinking of home and the Marseillaise, stumbling held back.
"Men we have won. We ex-slaves are victorious, defying Napoleon beyond the blue waves,
God gave us liberty, God gave us freedom. Shall we be slaves?"
Then from the throats of the wounded and dying, women and children, mingling their cry,
There rose like one breath in exultant hoarse sobbing,
  "Not till we die"!

When Dawns that Day

When dawns that day when Negro blood and brain and power shall hold dominion o'er the earth,
I want my race, my beautiful black race to prove its worth.

Say, "We the Negroes whom you tried to crush, to keep sub-
servient at life's lowest base,
Because we've suffered to make the world for you a better place,
Go plant your white feet firmly, face the sun unfettered,
Oh, swift white runners. Lift your eyes above. Behold God's
face."

Wishes

I want to be a great big man, like my daddy,
To eat big meat and rice, like my daddy,
To swing a big axe on my shoulder, like my daddy.
To cut through big mango trees till they fall 'Bang',
then shout 'Yoooooh', like my daddy.
To hew the logs and take them home for firewood, like my
daddy,
To say "Here, wife, wood for the fire", like my daddy.
To take a calabash full of palm wine and drink every
drop, like my daddy.
To sleep in the shade, sleep long, like my daddy.

I want to be a lovely woman, like my mammy,
With a smooth black shiny skin, like my mammy.
With many beads round my wrists and ankles, like
my mammy,
To cook white rice and stews that make one say 'Maaaa', like
my mammy.
So that when I go down to the waterside to wash, the birds and
lizards and stream will say,
"Here steps a lady, a lady like her mammy."

See also:
African Brownie song (Chapter Three)
My African hymn (Chapter Nine)
Nancy (Poems written for children)
Nativity (Chapter Three)
Rejoice (Chapter Two)
The serving Girl (Chapter Three)
The souls of Black and White (Chapter Three)
To the late Dr.Aggrey (Chapter Two)

Poems Inspired by
the Gold Coast(Ghana) & her People

Anamabu Tribal Motto

We men of Anamabu
Are possessed of the will to do,
And the mind to know how to do;
And the grit and the wit to do it well, whatever it is we do,
And the power to hold to the dream we have,
And make that dream come true.

We carry our water in baskets,
With a kata* of thorns on our heads.
We drink from the sieves the waters of ancient river beds.
Tenacity of purpose is ours as the linguist sings,
We do whatever we mean to do;
 We do the impossible things.

We men of Anamabu
Are possessed of the will to do,
And the mind to know how to do;
And the grit and the wit to do it well, whatever it is we do,
And the power to hold to the dream we have,

And make that dream come true.

A pad to cushion the head when carrying heavy loads on it.

Ashanti Tribal Motto

Here's the Ashanti motto: "Unconquerable from birth,
For every thousand slain, a thousand more spring from the
earth."

We are the men of the hottest blood,
We are the men who fight.
We are the giants, the vigorous men;
We are the men of might.
Ours the warm strength of the sun God made,
Ours is the speed of the winds,
With decisions clean cut like the keenest blade,
Ours are the mighty minds.

Ours is the claim to the ancient race,
Ours is the hard won fame,
Ours is tradition, song power, love grace,
Ours through Nyakupon's* name.

Here's the Ashanti motto: "Unconquerable from birth,
For every thousand slain, a thousand more spring from the
earth."

Nyakupon = God.

Getting up

Wink a little,
Blink a little,
Scratch your wee brown nose,
Yawn a little,
Sigh a little,
Snuggle 'neath the clothes.

Wink a little,
Blush a little,
Laugh and shake your head,
Rub your wee
Brown toes together,
Tumble out of bed.
Stand on both feet,
Slightly swaying,
Like twin flower stems,
Wild sweet Fantee piccanniny,
One of Afric's gems.

Lullaby

Close your sleepy eyes, or the pale moonlight will steal you,
Else in the mystic silence the moon will turn you white.
Then you won't see the sunshine, nor smell the open roses,
Nor love your Mammy any more, whose skin is dark as night.
You will only love the shadows, and the foam upon the billows,
The shadow of the vulture's wings, the call of mystery,
The hooting of the night owl, and the howling of the jackal,
The sighing of the evil winds, the call of mystery.
Wherever moonlight stretches her arms across the heavens,
You will follow, always follow, till you become instead
A shade in human draperies, with palm fronds for your pillow,

In place of Mammy's Bibini *asleep on his wee bed.

* ' *Bibini* ' *is Fante for a baby boy.*

Moonlight in Axim

Soft glimmers now the evanescent Moon
Slow, steal soft shafts of light, through lone dark trees;
Wearied, complaining, fretting, the sad sea
Moans still her grievance to the midnight breeze.
Spirits melt back to vapour, though they mock
The eerie crowing of the sleepy cock,
Dissolving brush-frail garments in their speed,
Against the watchdog, whimpering on the lead,
Who, barking in a frenzy of wild fear,
Snatches in vain at nothing, except air.

Seccondee Market

Through the deserted market place at night I strode,
Conscious of my own footfall rung from stones;
Aware that Terror on his wild steeds rode
Rattling his castanets of dead men's bones.
I stumbled against some stray dogs in my haste.
Dumb friends who own my love in broad daylight,
Howled with distrust, and peered into my face,
Then slinking off, became dissolved in night.
I who am fearless, feared this cold still place,
Ran, ran fleetfooted, sandaled by swift fright.

Through the thronged market place at noon I strode,
Pushed by the jostling crowd whose ready wit
Sprinkled with laughter which, preponderous, rolled

With mild sarcasm perforating it.
There sauntering midst its bizarre colour scheme,
Laughing, I paused a moment, wandering why
This same place, void of substance like a dream,
Rearing its haunting blackness to the sky,
Robbed of the moon's white penetrating beam
Strikes terror in the midnight passer by.

The Spirit of Axim

The hills asleep lay wrapped in purple mist,
Through which the dawn subdued, and fragrance kissed
Curled and uncurled, along the valley's rim -
Like vapour, passed the Spirit of Axim.
Hurtled through palm trees, fall the whetted blades,
Of lightnings, belched forth from depths of Hades;
Whilst the rain poured its sacrificial hymn -
Like thunder, passed the Spirit of Axim.

Who breathes through Appollonians* at their birth,
Love, peace, hate, death, and freedom of the earth?
Who quaffs Eternity, unto Life's brim -
Like mystery, passed the Spirit of Axim.

A name given to one of the oldest groups of Fante people

The Surf

Of song and moans and laughter, of danger there's no dearth,
As we come rolling home, pitching home, tossing through the
surf.
Blue is the sky above, of a deep blue-green is the sea,
And the thundering shock of wave against rock,

Crashes out loudly, 'We're free!'
The billows roar, the distant shore is threaded in shimmering gold,
The sun is a burning cloak; and the fingers of death are cold.
But love and youth are sweeter than ruth, and some of us lads are old.
So pull away, pull away, pull away lads, of strength there is no dearth,
As the nose of the boat shoots through the waves and we rock home through the surf.

The nets are cast, the boat is fast, the shimmering catch is hauled at last,
So out with your paddles and pull for home before the shadows begin,
When phantom hosts, with phantom boats draw souls of wanderers in.
Kwaku and Kwamina, Atta and Ekor fall into place again, balance that side.
Kwesi you take the helm, Kojo you paddle, let the boat songs echo out far and wide.
Ready boys! Steady boys! Bend to your labour, think of the women and children at home.
Sing aloud! Sing boys! Sing to drown danger! prove yourselves masters of hell-seething foam.
Bale out the water you two, keep clear-headed, watch
Paddle too soon or too late, and we are swamped, boys, then God have mercy on each weeping wife.
Ewuradzi Nyakupon, Great God of our fathers, steady our bobbing craft, temper our skill.
All through the ages the fierce raging elements own Thy Supremacy, bow to Thy will.
Sing boys, sing softly, pull, lads, pull gently, out of the gloom you can see the land rise,

Sweat beads our bodies, winds kiss our foreheads, tears of relief
gleam in dark shining eyes.

Oh, red is the sky above as sunset bathes the sea,
Hearts are raised in silent whispers, "Thank God we are free. Free
to live a little longer, free to love a little more,
Free to face a few more dangers, As we pull out from the shore."
Of song and moans and laughter, of danger there's no dearth,
When we come singing home, paddling home, tossing through
the surf.

See also:
Brown Baby Cobna (Chapter Eight)
The Palm Wine Seller (Chapter Three)

Poems inspired by
Sierra Leone & her People

Aberdeen

Aberdeen, oh Aberdeen, blue your transient waters,
Siren of twice twenty streams, where are our sons and daughters?
Devil of twice twenty worlds, why do you beguile them,
Take their living loveliness, kiss, strangle, kill, then hide them.
Every year a life is lost, in your sands uncurling
Like living snakes whose poisonous fangs are tiny currents
swirling.
Aberdeen, oh Aberdeen, blue your transient waters,
Siren of twice twenty streams, where are our sons and daughters?

The inspiration for this poem is an age-old belief in Sierra Leone that water
spirits sometimes abduct young people and kill them.

Character Sketch

Slanting eyes black as sloe,
Two curves for a mouth like a cupid's bow.
Two dark brown question marks for ears
And a bosom deep as the vale of tears.
Soft rounded arms, arched delicate feet,
With the slender charm of her hands compete.
A lappah* of blue, and a bubba** of red,
And a yellow silk handkerchief crowning her head.
Oh the innocent lure of her beckons and pleads
To the musical chink of her hidden beads.

lappah = wrapper

Freetown

Freetown when God made you, He made your soil alone
Then threw the rich remainder in the sea.
Small inlets cradled He, in dull black stone,
Wee bays of transient blue, He lulled to sleep
Within jet rocks, filled from th'Atlantic deep.
Then God let loose wee harbingers of song.
He scattered palms profusely o'er the ground
Then grew tall grasses, who in happy mirth,
Reached up to kiss each palm tree that they found.
"This is my gem," God whispered.   "This shall be
To me a Jewel in blue turquoise set."
Thus spoke the mouth of Life's Eternity,
There tranquilly lies Freetown even yet.
Then God couched lion-like, each mighty hill
Silent, they keep their watch o'er Freetown still.

Joseph's Betrothal

"Your garden grows a rose, " his people said.
"Yes", Mary's father raised his old white head.
"We have a rose," he answered, and his face
lit with love's light poured radiance o'er the place.
"We wish to pluck that rose that it may grow
Henceforth in Joseph's garden."   "Aye, I know,"
Lisped Mary's father, deeply sunk in thought.
"Transplanting of a rose is always fraught
With danger.   Who knows if fresh soil
Will nurture it as ours, with skilful toil?
Will love smooth out its petals, shade from sun,
Water when thirsting, tended by your son?"
"My son will tend it, it will bloom more rare,
This rose of yours, entrusted to our care."
Thus did they toss the matter to and fro,
The parents of the two in sunset's glow.

The poet is imagining a betrothal between Joseph and Mary that follows the
traditional custom among the Creoles of Sierra Leone.

Kissy

A bend within the wooded vales, set deep within a
frame
Of dark green hills a village blooms, and Kissy is its
name.
The church stands fair and beautiful, all houses turned that way,
To see the beauty gathered up when people go to
pray.

I think that God accepts it, and scatters it once
more
About the vales, streams, glades and hills of Kissy's
dew-drenched floor.
A bend within the wooded vales, deep set within a
frame
Of dark green hills a village blooms, and Kissy is its
name.

Lumley Beach

A sudden quiet as the car stood still.   A quiet in which

The dull roar of the sea, the thudding waves, the subdued
swishing of the ebbing tide,

Swift rushing Air, beating her wide-spread wings, the rustling of
green grass intensified.

So many visions focused through the sight, a perfect miniature
which memory frames.

The pouring radiance of the sun's white light, impressions far too
fragile even for names.

A skirt of grey foam curling round the strand.   Blue tossing waves
that proudly shoreward ride,

Stretch of tinted green o'er golden sand.   The wrecked *Fulani*
floating with the tide.

Clouds of pure white in the sun's brilliance hung.   Black rocks
pool-filled, ignored the roaring surf.

Tall palm trees bending o'er them gently swung by cradling wings
that tread the bright green turf.

One felt a great pure Presence breathe unseen, then glided
onwards till there came in view

Grey barks of palm trees crowned in tufted green, fringing the
winding road to Aberdeen.

Sunset o'er King Jimmy (Freetown)

Sunset o'er King Jimmy!
The sun slowly slipping like a veil from the dark
hill's brow,
Gliding over the valley, gilding each canoe's prow,
Nestling awhile on the palm trees, flecking the roofs
with gold,
Wrapping the sky in riotous colours, fold upon fold;
Kissing the sighing winds, kissing them till they weep,
Leaving them comfortless alone, vanishing into the deep.
Sunset o'er King Jimmy!

The Chief of Kitchom

Down to the Government wharf the Chief of Kitchom came,
Direct descendant of the line that reigns in Kitchom's name.

His face was like a hawk, his eyes were bright and keen,
His mouth a twist of irony, his smile swift cut and clean.

His pride sat on his brow like broad philactary,
His royalty like bands of steel girt round his dignity.

His gown was gara* blue, his red fez bound with white,
Nested each charm and prayer encased in leather from our sight.

He looked a tower of strength, his muscles easy played,
Rippled beneath his jet black skin with every step essayed.

His fingers gleamed with rings, his feet were sandal shod,
Girdles and chains hung round his neck, his strong hand held a
sword.

Thus Kitchom's naked blade gleamed in the setting sun,
And Kitchom's drums with throbbing beats mingled their tones
as one.

Thirty slim, dark brown girls stepped to the water's side
Behold the great Chief's wives they said, for each had been a
bride.

A great crowd pressed about, whilst from the boat's shaped stern
Soft music poured from balanges, as water from an urn.

Put out, away to the west. We breast the open main.
The Chief of Kitchom has been from home and now returns
again.

The boat is a tiny speck. We stand on the quay alone,
Whilst the sun breaks its red aureole, o'er the Chief who is going
home.

    * indigo dye

The Little Creole Boy

This morning through my window
A quaint old ditty rang.
I did not know the singer,
Nor the melody he sang;
But I thought of sturdy saplings,
O currents swift and wide,
Of strength and running laughter,
Of fresh blown limbs beside,
Of feet more brown than berries,
Of hair more black than night,
Of eyes as brilliant as new stars,
Of little teeth snow-white.
Of small brown chest expanded,
With bursts of song held fast
In the circle of his ruddy lips
Then trembling loose at last,
In trills and tuneless cadences
With little runs of joy,
A care-free ditty caroled
By a little Creole boy!

Written in Rotifunk Church (The Building)

The walls of the Church of Rotifunk are pure simplicity,
Of a pale, pale pink its upward reach, and below, the moss on a
tree.
The ceiled strong arch of Rotifunk Church is wide and high, and
free,
Like the freedom love brings to the heart of man, and a sense of
liberty.
The doors of the Church at Rotifunk are always open wide,
That whosoever wearieth can quietly step inside.

The pews of the Church of Rotifunk are carved with the strong
fine arm;
The world's greatest Carpenter wielded the saw, and helpedto
fashion this charm.
The bell of the Church of Rotifunk chimes out on the morning
air,
Its echoes fill the countryside, calling all men to prayer.
Within the garden that skirts the church, silence and
beauty meet,
The turmoil drops from the tired mind with the dust
of the outer street.
God bless the Church of Rotifunk, thus may it open stand
As a symbol that love is wider, far, than the sea, the sky and the
land.

See Also
To my little friends (Chapter Three)
Courtship (Poems written in Krio)
Dinner Time (Poems written in Krio)
In harbour {Freetown} (Chapter Eight)
Mende Kanya (Poems written in Krio)
Tunde(Poems written in Krio)

Poems Inspired by Nature

Adornment

With a slender comb of gold
The Night binds up her hair;
Then mortals say, "Behold,
The dawn is fair".
With a wine red dressing gown
She wraps herself about;

Then mortals say "Behold
The sun has come out".

Then when the fair Night dons
Her silver shoe,
Lo mortals say, "Behold
Day breaks anew".

Ariel

The secrets of the green grass and wild rose
Are secrets that the laughing Ariel knows.
He knows the rainbowed brilliance of each cloud;
He knows the night moth sleeps, he makes its shroud.
He reads the tides, he rides the crystal waves,
Holds speech with mermaids in red coral caves.
Each of these subtleties made Ariel's form,
His strength the force of wild waves in a storm,
Illusiveness is of his soul a part,
A dream's sad whimsicality his heart.

The Storm

It's a frightened sky today,
And a weeping sky as well,
The wind whirls by, in a frenzied way,
Straight from the mouth of hell.
The earth is struck by the storm's wild blight,
And the face of the sky is white, pure white.

It's a frightened sea today,
A swirling grey-coiled doom,
White, sheer white is the venomous spray,

It's no longer a sea but a tomb.
The boats that left our quays now sway
Engulfed in its awful gloom.

It's a frightened forest today,
Where mighty armaments crash,
And huge limbs reel in the wild affray
As in tournament they clash,
Whilst the pouring rain, with a moaning lay,
Washes each riven gash.

It's a frightened sea, a frightened sky,
And frightened lances hurled,
In a frenzied battle, 'twixt earth and sky,
Over a frenzied world.

To You Daisies

To you tiny woodland daisies, dotted on the summer grass,
Just to give you your due honour, I do curtsey as I pass.
For there are queens among the simplest, as with those
They may step through massive portals, also through a rustic gate.
If you're only pure and noble, and you stand up for
the right,
You're a queen of Love's own liking, though you may not dwell
in might.
Thus, you tiny woodland daisies, dotted on the summer grass,
Though the Rose be Queen of Summer, yet I curtsey as I pass.

See also:
A Dying Wish (Chapter Nine)
My Second Poem (Chapter One)
The Glorious World (Chapter Nine)

Poems Written for
Children & the Young at Heart

African Nursery Rhyme

The Harmattan is blowing, over vale and mound
And plucking mango leaves till they flutter to the ground,
Swaying, swaying,
Swaying, swaying,
Swaying, swaying, and fluttering to the ground.

The Ant

 I met the daintiest little Ant,
Her waist was slim and narrow,
"I wonder if you've bones? " I asked,
"And are they full of marrow?
Where are they situated,
Is what I'd like to know,
And are they lubricated,
Like people's bones, or no?
Surely you must have a skull,
Protection for your brains,
To know the rate, and the exchange
Of market goods and gains!"
But by the time I'd finished
My wonderful oration,
My dainty Ant, distinctly bored,
Had changed her situation.

The Kingfisher

A kingfisher sat in the pouring rain,
'Tu re la la, la lu!'
His poor little heart was bursting with pain
'Tu re la la, la lu!'
His beak was broken from flamboyant flower,
His feathers a deep sea blue,
Rimmed by the night in his birthday hour
Nobody could he woo.

His red beak flamed on his breast of grey
Caught from the mists of dawn.
'Will nobody love me, just for today?
Tu re la la, la lu, le lay,
The poor little bird did mourn!
But only the rain to his song gave ear,
And mingled its sorrow - tear for tear.

The Leaf

"I am still alive, I cling to my parent branch"
A young leaf was crying.
"I am still
            Flying,
                    Flying,
                            FLYING.'
But the night wind caught her and held her soft
He had chilled her heart.
She was
            Dying,
                    Dying,
                            Dying.

The Lizard

I met a handsome lizard, upon the gravel walk,
And so I stopped politely, and asked him for a talk.
He nodded once, he nodded twice, to make his meaning plain,
Glanced up at me with wee bright eyes, and nodded once again.

I said "You live on flies. Do you eat them alive or dead,
And when you eat them do they still keep buzzing in your head?"
He shrugged, then very haughtily inclined me to his ear,
Insinuating it was time I made my meaning clear.
"I'm sorry", I began, "but please, this question if I may;
Why? sure you shake your head for me, and nod your head for aye?"

He glanced at me with cold disdain, ignoring me, until
He slowly and deliberately climbed on the window sill;
He turned, he nodded, once, twice, thrice, to make his meaning plain,
Glanced up at me with wee bright eyes, and nodded once again.

The Mosquito

I detect melodious buzzing that prefaces attack;
It penetrates my snoring when I'm lying on my back.
I sit eyes shut a moment, my senses half awake,
I stretch out for my slipper; for my life is then at stake.
I light a sputtering candle - see, it hovers on the wing;
One mighty swipe, I hold my breath, I've missed the blessed thing.
Zing, bong, relentless my pursuit: I swear that it shall die.

Crash! I've hit it? No, I've missed it. Drat the beastly fly.
Hush! Like a supplicant I crawl upon my hands and knees
To where my enemy's ensign flaps in the midnight breeze.
Wallop! I see seven stars at once, a bump swells on my head,
Jug overturned, bed upside down, but the mosquito? - Dead!

Nancy

"Nancy, Nancy, where are you going?"
"Down to the bubbling brook to wash my clothes!"
"How will you know the direction, Nancy?"
"I shall hear the brook singing and follow my nose".
"What will you do when you get there, Nancy?"
"Wade into the stream, when I've climbed down the slope."
"And what will you do in the stream then, Nancy?"
"Soak the clothes well, then I'll rub them with soap."
"But what will you do when you've soaked them, Nancy?"
"I shall beat them with my patta*;   I shall rub them,
Dub them, scrub them, and bleach them in the sun!"
"Then what will you do when you've done that, Nancy?"
"Rinse them, and dry them. Then my work is done!"

* *a short paddle used for beating dirt out of laundry*

Politeness

At eight we say, 'Good morning,'
At noon we say, 'Good day,'
At three we say, 'Good afternoon,'
As we pass on our way.
But when the darkness deepens,
And little stars shine bright,
Then we say,' God bless you, and Good night.'

The Vulture

The vulture's the untidiest bird that I have ever seen;
His nails are always dirty, his mouth is seldom clean.
He wears his waistcoat crooked, then he forgets his tie,
He wears his top coat inside out, and winks a lazy eye,
Then ogles up with flattery, whenever you pass by.
One sees from the whole jumble of clothing that he wears,
He sleeps without undressing, and he never says his prayers.
The vulture never has the time for a refreshing bath,
But muddles through its filth and dirt and never has a laugh.
The vulture's the unhappiest bird that ever lived, I ween;
No home, no friends, no people, and a heart unclean, unclean.

See also:
Anatomy (Chapter Three)
Dinner Time (Poems written in Krio)
Mende Kanya (Poems written in Krio)
The Palm Tree (Chapter Three)

Poems Inspired by Spiritual Reflections

A Paean of Poets

My God, we thank Thee for the gift of song,
The struggle to existence which it brings;
Its great emancipation, its strong chains,
Its open losses, and its secret gains.
The soaring heights, the depths more deep than Hades
Which those who soar must sink to; where the glades
Are all tear flooded, where the willow trees

Grown by Despair moan in an anguished breeze.
We joy in fragile rose leaves still uncurled
Half living in a strange dream-peopled world.
Knowing that every paean that springs up starts
From our own beings, blood crimsoned from our hearts.
Then. oh, Great Inspiration, be thou near.
Flood through the channels of each open mind,
Cleanse us all through with Thy grace-bearing wind;
Till song be tempered by fresh purity
Sifted by love, then sung for all mankind.

A Woman's Prayer

God fill my eager empty yearning heart
With all-devouring love whose purged strong flame
Glows with a purpose fixed as stars,
Till "Union of two souls" becomes love's name.

God fill my eager being with the breath
Of new life stirring gently 'neath my heart,
Returning from the swinging gates of death,
Two beings instead of one who walked apart.

God fill my eager yearning tender arms
With love's supreme fulfilment, crowning bliss,
A crumpled rose leaf mouth, warm at my breast,
Small storms to hush, and little limbs to kiss.

God bless the little human trinity
The man, the wife, their crowning joy, the child,
Striving to reach their soul's divinity,
Through a pure home, all hallowed, undefiled.

Adagio

My heart beats like a melancholy tune,
Writ in slow tempo in a minor key,
Unutterably desolate in sadness.
Unless God changes the time signature,
Composing a new major melody,
Despairing of all faith, hope, love and gladness,
Unutterably desolate in sadness,
My wailing heart will moan itself to sleep,
In death's orchestral minor symphony.

Divine Design

I am steeling your heart with pain,
I am drilling it deep with tears,
That experience may be your gain,
To fight the advancing years.

I am scorching your heart with fire,
In life's crucible burning its dross,
That a purging of thought and desire,
May recompense all earthly loss.

I am swinging your heart into space,
Rocked alternate by life and by death,
That your soul may be strengthened to live,
When your body is robbed of its breath.

Reasonae

So that I might return to Him again,
God flayed me with the whip that men call pain.
So that my faith in Him would show no fears,
God drowned me in the well that men call tears.
So that I'd yearn for peace with Him above,
God cut me with the blades that men call Love.

Requiem

Thank God for my small, soft bed, clean and sweet
and white,
For the kindly shadows merging cool day into night.
For my mother's tender kiss and the waning light;
Angels guarding overhead to brush away cold fright.
Life-invigorating sleep, to renew my might.
Gathering strength to meet the day, continue with the fight,
For breathing space in which my soul can set itself aright,
For visions dreamy-sweet, the gift of sleep's
great sight,
For blest oblivion from day's cares which suddenly
take flight,
I thank Thee God.

Aged Twenty-Three

Sans Amore

Without love, I am like a voice without tone or melody.
Without love, I am like a rose bereft of colour and perfume.
Without love, I am like a vine whose support is taken away.

Without love, I am a beating pulse without warmth, impulse
without motive power, sense without intuition, strength without
control,
Therefore, without love, I am nothing.

Vesper

Lord of Light and all creation, hear us at the close of day,
Pardon every transgression, take, oh, take our sins away.
Grant us rest and peaceful slumber, when we close our eyes in
sleep,
Grant us blessings without number, safely till the dawn light keep.

Virtue

It is no virtue to be pure of speech,
When nought but noble things round thee are spoken;
It is no virtue ne'er to break an oath,
When round about thee ne'er an oath is broken;
It is no virtue not to lie or cheat,
When all around you deal in honest labour;
No virtue, strong temptation to defeat
When you ne'er feel its breath, nor taste its savor;
It is no virtue if your love is pure
With highest love around about you breathing;
No virtue to admit life through your door,
If you don't feel its pulse within you seething.
'Tis virtuous to buffet Life's rough sea
Which tries your soul's morality to sever,
Plough through the waves! Rise! Shake your timbers free!
Cry your defiance, laughing Never! Never!

Yema Lucilda Hunter

See also:
A Prayer (Chapter Nine)
Inspiration (Chapter Nine)
Nativity (Chapter Three)
The Harper's Prayer (Chapter Two)

Poems Inspired by the Joys,
Pains & Dangers of Love & Desire

A Vision of Love

Love came to me a sweet-eyed woman;
and her face was very beautiful. Her form was fair,
a dream herself, cloaked with dreamy hair.
A gentle dream-like softness was her robe,
A quiet unhurried restfulness her feet,
A depth of sweet contentment were her eyes.
Heaven curved her lips and arched her smile.
She vanished.

At night my guest returned, but now her tread
Beat on my heart till it lay still, lay dead.
Her hair as she bent o'er me brushed my breast,
She woke my heart to turbulent unrest.
Her eyes were far too sweet, their gaze too bold,
Her loosened robe let loose each mad desire.
Hell curved her lips, so dazzling was her smile.
I swooned, but in the dawn Love came to me,
A sweet-eyed woman, very beautiful,
A dream herself, cloaked in dreamy hair,
A gentle dream-like softness were her robes,
A quiet unhurried restfulness her feet,

184

A depth of sweet contentment were her eyes.
Heaven curved her lips and arched her smile.
She vanished.

Awakening

I wake at dawn, and know that e're the dusk
Has purple shadowed all the rim of earth,
Some golden hour, joy winged, because it must
Bear you upon it thus increase its worth,
Will bring you unto me. Then I shall hear
Your feet beat out the rhythm of your tread;
And trace again your open countenance
Framed by the glossy hair curled o'er your head.
I know that I shall hear the soft half tones
That modulate to blend and form your voice,
And catch your glance as conversation curls
Its gleaming threads about us.   I rejoice
Because I am all love, and nought of fear,
All tenderness, all pain, when you are near.

Comfort at Dawn*

I woke to find my pillow wet with tears;
The soft warm hush was very, very still.
No rain-kissed wind lips brushed my burning mouth,
No perfume breathed upon me from the South,
No shadows laid their cheek against my cheek,
Would no one comfort me? Would no one speak?
Even the eyes of sleep were steeped in dew.
"I, Night, will watch with you," the warm Night said.
She pillowed on my breast her dusky head.

But ere dark hollows were suffused with light,
I heard the sweet deep breathing of the Night.
"Would no one comfort me?"
Dawn heard - she gently came,
Soothed me to sleep, by breathing - just - your name.

Defiance

I will never yield to you, never,
Desire's incarnate son.
You staked on the flesh and lost.
I staked on the spirit, and won.

Though you blot out the beauty of night
And the stars that gleam in the skies,
Are reduced to the passionate burning
Of the orbs of your piercing eyes;

Though the humid warmth of the night
That through the window slips
Seems to my reeling sense
The touch of your finger tips;

Though the fragrant laden dew
Of our sunny beautiful south
Is not sweet as the fragrant moisture
Of your clinging passionate mouth;

Though the wind that ruffles the curtains
And blows through the delicate air,
Is like your strong hands stirring
Very gently through my hair;

Though the night be reduced to hunger
Of a burning flame,
And time but the iteration
That beats your name;

I will never yield to you, never,
For in seeking your ultimate goal,
You forgot the essence of God
Alive in each human soul.

Purity wins in the end
Though I'm caught in your tangled mesh;
Who cannot hold my spirit,
Never shall win my flesh.

Distance

Distance has robbed me of so many things
That make humdrum existence very dear.
The sun no shadow on the pathway flings
As certainty that you are somewhere near.
No longer may I raise the curtain frill
And gaze expectant at the crowd below
With a delicious sweet ecstatic thrill,
To watch unseen, beloved, where you go.
No longer may I startled wake from sleep
Your name from my lips dropping like sweet dew
To curb my hungry longing, let it keep,
Knowing the morrow's dawning will bring you.
No longer may I lift my warm face up
For your soft kiss, pressed down upon my lips.
This is the yearning which we women feel
Prone wanderers who sail the seas in ships.

And yet with all this anguish, had you wings,
Soul whom I love, I would not have you here.
Distance has robbed me of so many things
That made life's dull monotony so dear.

My Secret*

I shall love you always, not matter what befall,
But I must keep my secret, and wait until you call.
But when you call, beloved, like a bird in flight,
With the swiftness of the storm, with the haste of night,
With the cooing of a dove, the humming of a bee,
Straight homeward will I come, beloved, unto thee.

With the strength of the lion, the weakness of the deer,
The confidence of warriors, the captive's fear,
The laughter of gladness, the sorrow of tears,
The archness of youth, and the wisdom of years,
With my heart palpitating in my eager breast,
Straight homeward will I fly - there find me rest.

If You Should Come to Me

If you should come to me with heart aflame
With love and joy, at mention of my name,
Then would I bow in worship at your feet,
Love would be full, and life would be complete.
But come not unto me through pity deep,
To wipe my tears because you know I weep.
Far rather would I die than have it said,
"He came through pity when his love was dead."

Insomnia*

By day thoughts cross the checker-board of my mind,
In orderly array, moved by control.
They meet, advance, retreat, checkmate and slay,
Conquering and stilling my subconscious whole.
But when sleep comes, your name, your dear, dear name,
Hidden too deep for consciousness to reach,
Pours its swift stream through all my restless blood,
Surges right through the silence, breaks in speech
Till with a moan the dam bursts into flood.
Then love, my intense longing, and your name,
Lights darkness with love's trinity of flame.
Onward emotion rushes; in a flash
Your form is focused on my lens of pain.
Love turns the undeveloped negative
Into a finished portrait in my brain,
Which nothing can eradicate again.

Let Silence Speak

I am breathless when I behold you so radiantly pure and fair;
My spirit leaps forth to enfold you, and all the
enchanted air,
Is full of the magic cadence of the feathered nightingale's throat,
And my heart is so full of singing, that it spills not a
single note.
Like a nesting bird that is homing, straight unto you I
come;
Let silence speak and plead my cause, for love has rendered me
dumb.
Love plucks the quivering heart strings, and turns them into a
lute.
Let love now speak for itself, for love has rendered me mute.

Love's Logic

Your love is far more noble, dear, than mine,
You worship the ideal instead of me;
When you and I are spirit, when the brain
Grasps being without form eternally
Then shall I let dear human symbols die,
Love gloriously the spirit you will be.

Living, I love the fragrant wholesome man.
Your virile strength is poignant ecstasy.
Your hands that sketch swift meaning are more dear
Than that internal being I cannot see.
Your eyes sufficient truth to make me know
That in your love held bondage I am free.

I love your boyish laugh, your sullen moods,
The clean swift animation of your face;
I love your close cropped hair, whose tiny curl
Scrambles confusedly about; I love the grace
With which you turn to make for me a smoother place.
I love the living you that now draws breath,
If God permit, I'll love you thus till death.

The gentle trembling fingers straightening out
My ruffled collar, or my cuffs of lace,
The rough smell of your clothes, a hundred things
That love alone in voice and mood can trace.
You love your great ideal in me, you say,
But I, being woman, love the simpler way.

My Beloved

He is coming, my beloved,
Love is borne upon the air,
From his radiant noble spirit,
To my heart, to nestle there.

He is coming through the sunshine,
Swift his manly, dusky feet;
But the hour of love's awakening
Is too full - yea, far too sweet.

He is coming through the bowers
Of hibiscus roses red,
I can feel him, in the flowers,
Where my love has laid his head.

I can feel him in the river,
Where he cometh oft at noon;
Lilies tremble at his beauty,
He departeth far too soon.

He is coming, his light footfall
Makes my weak heart dance and sing,
He is coming, when the dove's call
Greets the awakening cry of spring.

He is coming, in my spirit
In my fancy! Through my night,
He will come, he will not know me -
'Tis a dream - I have no sight.

My Lips

My Lips were buds of innocence until you came one day
And drew a fountain from my heart, and careless went your way.

My lips were hungry eager flowers curved in ecstatic bliss
To gather the soft sweetness of my next lover's lips.

My lips were luscious ripeness of a crushed and poisoned vine,
When you bent your lips upon me, and my soft ones clung to
thine.

My lips are withering fading flowers full weary unto death,
Dew without moisture is thy kiss, wind without heat, thy breath.

A fugitive tear wells up from my eyes, and is secretly,silently shed;
Are lips that once were innocent, so withered,
so parched, so dead?

Payment

I stooped to drink from a forbidden river,
But stopped because mud stirred beneath the gold.
Because my lips have touched it, now and ever,
I must repay a hundred thousand-fold.

Realisation

I did not know that you had the power to hurt me,
I think I must have bequeathed it to you unknowingly
One starlit night when I read the secret in your eyes.
Did you read mine? I know now that you did.

Use your power gently, beloved, for in your hand it
becomes a merciless whip.

I did not know that you had the power to make me happy.
I think I must have bequeathed it to you unconsciously
In the warm darkness when your lips met mine and pressed their
weight of love on them.
Did your soul leap to meet mine?   I know now that it did.
Use your power gently, beloved, lest in your hand it
grows too great for me.

Your Presence

When your presence hovers near me, worry and discord cease.
My heart throbs with delight, then lies quite still at peace.
When your presence hovers near me, I throw off the weight of
years,
My heart throbs well up in laughter, love's laughter tinged with
tears.
When your presence hovers near me, the skies grow blue above,
My heart throbs out its welcome with the quivering joy of love.

Warning

Pray do not love too well, dear, it is not over wise
To let desire run riot in your passion-filled dark eyes.
Suppose my heart caught fire from your ignited spark,
A flame of passion would result, illumining the dark.
The darkness of lost innocence would lay its awful pall,
Upon us both, beloved, and shame keeps us in thrall.
I'd glory in thus sinning; you bloom a thing apart.
You are so frail a flower, beloved, that it would break
your heart.

Be gentle with me, dearest; be loving, yet be wise,
Do veil the rioting sweetness of your love-filled, glorious eyes.
See also:
Advice (Poems written in Krio)
African love song (Poems inspired by Africa…)
Beat for me Sangbye beat (Poems inspired by Africa…)
Courtship(Poems written in Krio)
Love Me (Chapter Four)
Love's Clarion Call (Song Lyrics)
Rainy Season Love Song (Poems inspired by Africa…)

*Poems Inspired by Other Reflections,
Observations & Experiences*

A Code to Live By*

You must be full of the beauty of earth, of the sea and the land
and the sky.
And full of the wonder of man himself as a code to live life by.
And full of the mystery of love, and a faith that outshines the
stars,
And full of the strength of the pure in heart, to live this life of
ours.
To live midst its battle and hurry and strife, extortionate greed
and gain,
To unravel the psychological twist that knots up the human brain.
To live with a song in your pulsing throat, and a light in those
eyes so deep,
And the smooth firm touch of comforting hands,
when we finally break our mortal bands,
As we enter the vale of sleep.

Dawn

Dawn for the rich, the artistic, and the wise,
Is beauty splashed on canvas of the skies;
The brushes being the clouds that float the blue,
Dipped in the breeze for paint, and washed by dew.
But dawn to those who bathe the night in tears,
Squeeze sustenance from hard unyielding years,
Is full of strange imaginings and fears.
The dawn renews the terror of the day
Where harassing uncertainties hold sway;
And pain held in surcease through brief hours of rest
Rears up its head in its unceasing quest
To wear out body, brain, and mind and soul,
Till death is a resolve, and death a goal.
For these life holds no beauty, dawn no light,
For day is hopeless, dawn is struck with blight.

Dear, Familiar Things

I sing a song of dear, familiar things,
Things that the smallest child will understand,
The feel of winds that brush across the land,
The fluttering softness of the night moth's wings.
Wash of the salted spray whose indigo
Merges with green and shy familiar grey,
The glowing dawn, the silver, shimmering moon,
The loveliness that heralds each new day.
Girlhood and womanhood and blossoming birth
Swift, vigorous manhood recreating man,
Life's mystery no mortal man can scan,
Fair children replenishing old earth.

Babies - God bless the gurgling joy they crow;
Toddlers - a peck of trouble but how dear;
Rollicking boys and laughing girls whose cheer
Is faith in things above, and things below.
I sing a song of dear, familiar things,
Of all the common things that sum up life,
Threading their way through its tumultuous strife.
Things which occur in every age and clime,
Totalled by God and checked by hoary time.
Winds, waft my singing homeward with swift wings
Back to the hearts of dear, familiar things.

Folk

Do you know the hush folk?
The silent wheeling hush folk?
Mammoth moth and fire-fly,
Red bat and dragon fly,
Silent owl now circling by,
Do you know the hush folk?

Do you know the crush folk?
Lusty crags, with mighty claws,
Crumbling pits, with open jaws,
Beasts, with dripping blood-bathed maws,
Do you know the crush folk?

Do you know the blush folk?
Beauty breathing blush folk?
The blush folk we term "the rose",
Blush folk evening skies disclose;
Blush folk, which love breathes and glows,

Do you know the blush folk?

Do you know the mist folk?
Mystery-mantled mist folk?
Folded round the weeping skies,
Lurking, hid, in human eye,
Veiling warm earth, kissing-wise,
Do you know the mist folk?

Do you know the sleep folk?
Comfort-bearing sleep folk?
Cradlers of each living birth,
Closers of the eyes of earth,
Ministers of widest girth,
Do you know the sleep folk?

Indifference

The night was chill, chill dews lay on my lips,
Beaded my forehead, and a little wind
Blew sharp and clean, chilling my very bones;
Cold, I awoke. The cold stars chilly gleamed in the clear sky.
My very heart seemed chilled to living death.
I turned my head, behold a figure stood
Cold, motionless, alone, a vague disturbing void of
chilly draperies.
With a transparent hand she raised a veil.
No sound came from her lips, but from the air
"I am Indifference," fell.   My terror-stricken cries
Rang weirdly through the room, for lo!
Indifference had no eyeballs, and no eyes.

London Buses

I love the London buses, with their padded seats and springs;
And their brightly coloured posters on all sorts of different
things;
The winding iron stairway, with its glittering rails of brass,
And the gangway 'twixt the seats upstairs, down which people
pass.

I love to see the driver blow his horn, and shift his gears,
And watch men whisper secrets in tiny shell-pink ears,
And hear the laugh of children who make the grown-ups smile,
While the conductor names the stops at every quarter mile.
I love the London buses, for all who ride may see
The beauty of the sunset, the wold, the bud , the tree,
The buildings silhouetted against the sky of grey,
The crescent moon ascending the sky at close of day.
I love the London buses.

Song of the London Pavements

We are the London pavements and we always love to hear
The quick unsteady pattering feet of little children
dear.
The heavy, quick, determined tread of men who hold
Control
Of businesses, the thoughtful tread of men who savethe soul.
The springing, delicate, swift tread of those with
dancing toes,
The hearty "don't care" easy tread that every wanderer knows.
The wearied, dragging, tired feet of people who despair,
The haughty, proud, quick mincing steps of rich ones
who don't care.

The hesitant, uncertain tread of foreigners to town,
The loud, clod-hopping, rolling walk of agile Farmer
Brown.
The unrelenting tread of "Bobby" on the "Beat".
The furtive, cat-like, silent tread of robbers who
retreat.
And once in every thousand years like wind blown o'er the sod,
We bow in awe and worship as we feel the tread of God.

The Cart-Horse

When blue becomes intense and dusks to grey,
Grey unto darkness shrouding the worn day,
I like to lie awake and gaze upon the cloudless sky
And hear the song of the cart-wheels as the old cart-horse goes
by.
The squeaking boards
The rusty chains,
The clank of steel and brass,
The intermittent hoof-beats as the old cart-horse goes past.

When darkness turns to grey again and grey to light,
When little wrens awake prepared for flight,
I like to lie awake with the warm sun streaming in,
And try to understand the tune the good old cart-wheels sing.
The squeaking boards,
The rusty chains,
The clank of steel and brass;
Oh, I love to hear the music of the cart-horse going past.

The Stairs

When everything turns inside out, in spite of tears and prayers,
Just prop your chin in both your hands, and sit upon
the stairs,
Just sit down on the stairs.
Don't sit down in the middle, that's the halfway house of things,
Don't sit down at the bottom, when your feet have lost their
springs,
Or you'll lose the art of climbing unawares.
But cuddle in the corner, and just let things alone,
Let your poor head find a pillow 'gainst the woodwork and the
stone.
When sympathy just sheds the tears a-springing to your eyes,
When pity twists your heart in knots of anger and surprise,
And you hate the fools around you, and are bitter with the wise,
There's nothing then to ease you, or to cheer your heart's wild
strife,
But sitting there upon the stairs, and looking back at
life.
Then you see the steps you've mounted, past the obstacles in
view,
With the banister of Hope still standing, waiting there for you.
Though the step you're on blows chilly, it was colder at the base,
And you've triumphed over evils, you have not yet lost the race
But feel a bit discouraged that in spite of hopes and fears,
You don't seem to get much farther than just sitting on the stairs.
There's no need to feel discouraged, for the far end of the flight
Is flocked with stars and moonbeams that shed brilliance through
the night.
And you won't stay there forever, for the spirit that's in you
Is strong enough to suffer, to triumph, dare and do.
So when everything turns inside out, in spite of tears and prayers,
Just prop your chin in both your hands, and sit upon the stairs,

Just sit down on the stairs!

The Thief*

I wondered what bent my lilies white
Over the black-lipped bowl in which they stand
Like infants' snow-white prayers, for purity,
Fluttering on stalks of green, like stems of peace.
I watched.   Behold, an atom bird flew down,
Perched on the stems, and kissed each snow-white crown,
Its love thirst slaking, from the sweet that slips
Up from their white souls, to their fragrant lips;
They bowed themselves to him, in fond belief,
He flew away forgetful - cunning thief!

To Mother

Mother, before me lies the open road.
I know not where it leads, save deep into the mysteries of sweet
womanhood.
But I go forth assured that you have trod the path before, and
understood.
Sweet Mother, when I've passed the open door,
I'll know why you love me; thus shall I love you more.

To my Mother

Mother I need you. Though a woman grown,
My own self's arbitrator, my own law,
My need of you is deeper than I've known,
And far more urgent than it was before.
Into your tender arms I'd love to creep,

Pour out my woes, and cry myself to sleep.

But even were you here, this could not be,
Convention kills the sobbing child in me.
Since soft white luster crowned your smooth fair brow,
'Tis I, the child, turns mother to you now.
Then whilst my firm hand smoothes your long white hair,
And my young lips press from your eyes the tears,
Whilst my strong arms are round you, resting there in my
embrace, I lose the weight of years.
And when you smile, confiding tilt your head,
To gaze into my eyes, I'm comforted.

To my Mother (a sonnet)

Brown, low, broad brow, soft, deep set, amber eyes,
White, snow-white hair waved backward from her face
Whose pure serenity, like evening skies
Spreads its pervading peace through cloud-wrought space.

In shades of life, splashed silver dews of tears
Is her mouth painted by the brush of years,
Who mingles laughter in the line he dips
In the warm colouring of mother-lips.

Brown hands enmeshed by toiling to provide
Home, food, clothes, shelter for me till the end.
Brave spirit whose significance doth hide
Its subtlety in "Mother", treasured friend.

How can I read your lovely soul aright?
Its tenderness is endless, infinite!

Twenty-One

I am twenty one in the prime of youth,
Stern self accuser searching for truth,
Intolerant I look with scorn
On those whose minds seem lowly born.
With eager hand stretched out to grasp
My personality by the hasp
That opens the box of the infinite,
Exultant in my own strength and might,
I tread the earth. I do not stumble.
I plant firm feet on the edge of day,
Till the truth in my Mother's eyes renders me humble.
I bow down and worship, and know I am clay.

See also:

Poems Written in Krio

Krio was once spoken only by the Creoles of the Western Area of Sierra Leone, but has become the lingua franca of the entire country. Modern Krio orthography has been substituted for Gladys's hit or miss attempt at writing the language, which was all that was available at the time. Suitable Krio titles have also been suggested where she used English ones.

Guide to Pronunciation

Vowels

a - as in 'bat'.

e - as in 'play, they, neigh, make, wait', etc.

i - slightly longer than 'pig', but shorter than 'meet'.

o - as in 'go, woe, road, grow, old', etc.

u – as in 'put, you, who, good', etc.

Other speech sounds

ɛ - as in ' eh, wet', etc.

ɔ - as in 'jaw, dog', but more clipped.

aw - as in 'now, cloud', etc.

ay - as in 'hide, mind, eye, by,' etc.

ɔŋ – closest in English is ' song'.

Note: Consonants are pronounced as they are in English.

Advice (Tek advays)

"Go pre to Gɔd mi pikin, mek yu pul at kɔmɔt de;
Di man nɔ yus, mi pikin, lɛf am mek i go in we."
"Wetin fɔ do, mi sista, wɛn na so yu pipul se?"
A pre to Gɔd – nɔ bɛtɛ; na naw mi lɔv kan wɔs,
Ɛn Setan mek di ol lɔv kan ɔt naw pas di fɔs.
"Titi, jɛs sidɔn saful, wan gud man go aks fɔ yu."
Bɔt wɛn yu lɔv di bad man, sista; du ya we fɔ du?

Translation:

"Ask God to help you , my child, and you will be able to forget about him. He is a worthless man. Let him go."

"What can you do, sister, when your parents tell you something like that?"
I have tried praying, but it hasn't helped at all. Satan is making me love him even more.
" My girl, just relax. A good man will ask for your hand."
Yes, but when one loves the bad man, what is one to do?

Courtship (Yan swit)

I tinap; misɛf tinap te a put in kalbas dɔŋ.
A se, 'usay yu kɔmɔt, bo?"
"A kɔmɔt Fula Tɔŋ."
I sɛt in mɔt, mi sɛt mi mɔt; i tan lɛk spirit pas,
So te a drɔ am klos mi fɔ kam sidɔn na di gras.
Dɛn noto kɔmɔn yan wi yan. If yu yɛri we a de shut,
Waylst mi wan yay jɛs de spay am, frɔm in ed te rich in fut.
I luk mi; misɛf luk am. A se, "A lɛk yu,bo!"
I drap in swit yay wantɛm; i se, " Misɛf lɛk yu, Jo."
I kis mi; misɛf kis am. Na so mi at de bit.
Dɔn we tɛl gudbay. A wach am te i lɔs go dɔŋ di trit.

Translation:

I stopped and she too stopped. I put her calabash down.
I said, "Where have you come from?"
She said, "From Fullah Town"
I fell silent. She too fell silent as if a ghost just passed ; then I drew her close to me and we sat down on the grass.
 I gazed at her from head to toe, whispering sweet nothings in her ear in my bad English. You should have heard me!
She looked at me and I looked at her. I said, "I do love you".

She dropped her gaze at once but said, " I too love you, Joe."
She kissed me and I kissed her back. My heart was beating fast;
then we said goodbye. I gazed after her till she disappeared down
the street.

Dinner Time
(Tɛm Fɔ It)

"Jane, go pul di fufu. Ayɔ tɔn di pɔt.
Bɔbɔ, yu go was dɛm plet, mek di sup go ɔt.
Maria nɔ kam bak yet? Lɔ da pikin slo!
A jɛs sɛn am fɔ bay rɛs, frɔm lɔŋ tɛm we i go?
Sɔni de ple bɔl na trit. A tink se in de wet fɔ mek a kɔl am. A
nɔ ful. A bisin if i let?
Tunu, tɛl yu Sisi se if i nɔ go stɔp
Fɔ nak da piano bɔm, bɔm, bɔm, ɛn tray kam dɔŋ ɛn chɔp.
U ambɔg mi, nɔ go gɛt wan gren dray fish sɛf.
Jane, yu pas da kɔba dish we de pantap da shɛlf.
Ɔlman fɔ go was dɛn pan. Ɔlman tek dɛn spun.
I luk lɛk se una ɔl nɔ wan go skul dis aftanun.
Jane, Bɔbɔ, Tunu, Ayɔ, Maria, Sisi, Sɔni, Swit,
Se yu gres ɛn tek yu plet. Tɛl tɛnki, ɛn go it"

Translation:

"Jane, dish out the fufu, Ayo, stir the pot; and Little Boy, you
wash the dishes while the soup is being warmed. Maria isn't back
yet? Lord, that child is slow!! I just sent her to buy some rice, and
that was long ago. Sonny is still playing ball in the street,
expecting me to call him. I'm no fool. I don't care if he's
late…Tunu, go tell your sister to stop banging on that piano and
come down right now to eat. Anyone who bothers me, won't get

even a tiny piece of smoked fish – Jane, pass me the dish cover on that shelf – by now everyone should have a clean plate ready and a spoon. You're all behaving as if you don't want to go to school this afternoon. Jane, Little Boy, Tunu, Ayo, Maria, Sisi, Sonny, Sweet, say your grace, give thanks and eat."

Kongosa

Fɔ kip yu mɔt, mi sista, if yu wan mek biznɛs rayt.
Nɔ kongosa na mɔnin, nɔ tɔk dɛn se na nɛt.
I lɛk yu nak dɛn biba, gɛ digri, wɛr gawn ɛn ud,
Na skiakro yu go fiba, if yu kongosa, mi brɔda
 Bikɔs Kongosa nɔ gud.

Dɛn se kin bring big plaba; dɛn se wɔd nɛba tru.
Wɛn dɛn tɛl yu se na so dɛn se, na trap dɛn sɛt fɔ yu.
If yu nɔ gri kongosa, dɛn go go lay ɔda ples.
Noto yu go miks pan wahala ɛn trɔbul ɛn disgrɛs.

If wɔd de we yu mayn ɛn at, wan Pɔsin de fɔ tɛl.
Lɛf ɔl di we dɛn se gi Gɔd, i ɔndastan ful wɛl.
Bɔt nɔ go tɛl yu neba, if yu wan mek biznɛs rayt.
Nɔ kongosa na mɔnin, nɔ tɔk dɛn se na nɛt.

Translation:

Gossiping

Sister, don't gossip if you want things to go well. Don't gossip in the morning; don't utter 'They say' at night. My brother, even if you're a graduate with hood and gown, or a sophisticated dresser, you'll end up no better than a scarecrow, if you gossip, because gossiping is bad.

'They say', can cause huge quarrels, and 'they say' is never true. If someone tells you, 'That's what they say,' they are setting a trap for you. If you refuse to gossip they'll take their lies elsewhere, instead of leaving you open to problems and being shamed.

If you're longing to repeat some gossip, there's Someone you can tell. Leave God to deal with all 'They say', He knows people just too well. Please don't tell your neighbour if you want things to go well. Don't gossip in the morning, don't utter 'They say' at night.

Mende* Kanya**

Mende kanya swit - o!
Yu min se a de ple?
Mek di granat pach gud fashin,
Pak nɔf shuga de.

Mende kanya swit o!
Fɔ ayd am insay klas,
Dɔk yu ed ɛn mɔndɔ
Bifo yu ticha pas.

Mende kanya swit o!
Skul dez kin swit tu,
Bɔt jɛs yu dɔn big lilibit,
Dɛn plɛzhɔ dɔn fɔ yu.

Bay wan kɔpɔ yon,
Bay tu kɔpɔ yon,
Bay tri kɔpɔ yon,
Yu smok am ma!

* *Mende — one of the major ethnic groups in Sierra Leone*

**a snack made from roasted peanuts, ground and mixed with rice flour and sugar.*

Translation:

Mende Kanya is absolutely delicious. I'm not joking. Roast the peanuts very well and add enough sugar.
Mende Kanya is absolutely delicious. You should hide it in class, bob down and eat some when your teacher is unaware.
Mende Kanya is absolutely delicious. School days are good too, but as soon as you start growing up then pleasure is no more.
Buy a penny's worth, buy two pennies worth, buy three pennies worth and just *guzzle* it!

Tunde

Do dɔn klin,
Kak dɔn kro,
Lebra mɔni ɔl dɔn go.

Tunde rɛs pap swit fɔ it
Pas ɔl ɔda pap na trit.

Tunde yay i swit fɔ luk
Pas di pap we Tunde kuk

Pap dɔn dɔn, yu de wet;
Tunde u yu si na get?

Masi Tunde! dɔn yan du,
Mɔdɛnlɔ de wet fɔ yu.

Translation:

Day has dawned, the cock has crowed, and labourers are penniless.
Tunde's rice pap is most delicious, better than anybody else's on the street.
Tunde's eyes are even more irresistible than her pap.
Your pap is all sold out but you haven't come indoors, Tunde. I wonder what is keeping you.
Tunde, stop flirting, for goodness sake!
Your mother-in-law is waiting for you.

See also:

Take Um So (Notes on Chapter Eight)

Song Lyrics

A Rolling Stone

Cut me out of your thoughts, baby, with the close of this day,
'Cos a rolling stone don't gather no moss, and I must
To weather storm and sunshine, with my bed under swaying trees,
Feel the throb of screws on the quarter deck as I sail the heavy seas.

Chorus:

I never gather no money, I've never time for a friend,
I don't gather love or laughter, to sweeten my journey's end.
So it's goodbye, honey, forget me, there're plenty of folks in town,
If I can't roll up the hill with you, I must roll alone on

down.
Don't get wild, darling, don't get cross, 'cos a rolling stone don't
gather no moss.
I'm a rolling stone!

As Long as You're There

Any old time, or any old place,
It does not really matter where,
Nor any odds I have to face,
So long as you're there.

Life may hold its laughter,
Life may hold its tears,
Sweating 'neath the sun,
Toiling through the years,
What do I care? So long as you're there?
So long as you're there the skies are blue,
The flowers smell sweet, the doves all coo
And everything else except Love is new
So long as you're there.

If you should be taken, and I left behind,
I don't know how I should carry on here.
I'd work with my body, my soul and my mind,
To reach high Heaven, so long as you're there.
So long as you're there the skies are blue,
The flowers smell sweet, the doves all coo
And everything else except Love is new
So long as you're there!

Builder's song

From the play "Samuel" (male chorus).

Tie the sapling mango stakes stout and strong;
Cut them all of equal length,
Not too long.
Plait the slender supple palm
For the roof.
Thatch against all sun and harm
Waterproof.
Clay scooped from the river side,
Soft and red.
Fill cracks left by the stakes,
Mat for bed.
Doors and windows must not be
Slit to spy
Where your food can be let in
By and by.
Let the devil rage and foam,
Baffled quite;
He can never break your home,
Have no fright.
You are safe from every foe,
So goodnight.
Stars look down on him with love,
Lend your light.

Age Twenty Four

Blue days

Blue days flooded with sunshine and song birds' soft singing,
Blue days with laughter ringing, Oh, come back once more.
Sad days, mad days,
And wearying bad days,
Pack up your troubles and leave me,

Now that you've settled your score.
Blue days filled with the perfume of spring flowers growing,
Blue days with breezes blowing, Oh, come back once more.

But for you

But for you I would have been a failure,
Never faced my life and lived it through;
Never found the courage for existence,
Never deemed love could be found and true,
Never dreamed that dark clouds hide the sunshine
And that hope will break the gloom of night,
Never knew you'd be my guardian angel,
My true beacon and my soul's light.

April 12th, 1929.

Call Me

An African Boy and an African Girl stood by the forest rim
His head was bowed, his step was slow, and his eyes with tears
were dim.
He was a mighty warrior and she feared he might be slain,
Thus in a husky whisper she sang this soft refrain.

Chorus:

"Call me by the beating of the tom-toms, and I will hear;
Your love vibrating through its accents will echo clear.
Whether it be by plain or hill,
Love will guide my footsteps still.
I will come to the beating of the tom-toms.
Whether the moon be shining on high,

Whether fierce storm clouds darken the sky,
I will come to the beating of the tom-toms.
To its muffled sweet staccato beat
My eager, dark brown feet
Will skim the ground
And the rising mound till I come to you.
Call me, call me, call me to the beating of the tom-toms."

Following You

You are my beacon, you are my star,
I will hitch my wagon to you and follow where you are,
From the North and West and South and way back home again,
Motor car or buggy or boat or aeroplane.

Chorus:

I'll just keep following, following, following you around
I'll just keep on following, following you around,
Following, following, following you around.
Following you, only you, following you around.

Until you stop your climbing and notice me behind
My love song will come drifting to you, honey, on the wind.

I'll just keep following etc.

Hum a Bit of Melody

Humming is the easiest thing a man can do, I find.
One hasn't always got the heart to sing,

But you'll find things much brighter if you keep this thought in mind,
A little bit of humming sweetens everything.

Chorus:

So long as there's a crescent moon peeping o'er the hill,
Hum a bit of melody.....Hmmmmah

It shines there to remind you that God's in Heaven still,
Hum a bit of melody.....Hmmmmah

What if your heart is breaking, will crying set it right?
Hum a bit of melody; things will come out right.
Hum a bit of melody; never mind the tune,
Hum a bit of melody.....Hmmmmah

**I'm Out to Sit on the World
(So the world don't sit on me)**

Don't be so unhappy,
Don't be so blue,
Success is round the corner
She's waiting there for you.
Work a little harder, use more pep and grit,
You'll beat any trouble if you just stand up to it.
Here's a little motto, here's a little tune,
Sing it in December, whistle it in June:

Chorus:

I'm out to sit on the world, so the world don't sit on me.
I won't be bound by life's chains, my laughter shall set me free.

I'm ready for another bout,
Though life itself has knocked me out.
I'm out to conquer the world, so the world don't conquer me.

Love's Arithmetic*

I parted from the boy I love, and parting made me blue,
I know he feels unhappy and is yearning for me too.
For love has got its happiness and love has got its tears,
He sang this song to comfort me, and calm away my fears.
"You and I are two,
Love will make us one,
And from that one the baby which makes three.
Subtract from that all care, and nothing else remains
But joy and happy laughter, and love's sweet ecstasy.
You and I are two, but love will make us one,
And from that one the baby which makes three.
So never mind the sadness, there are days ahead of gladness,
In the total sum of love for you, dear, and for me."

Love's Clarion Call

Love's clarion call is sounding, over both hill and lea;
"Love and be loved to be happy, love and be loved to be free."
Love and be loved to be hopeful, brimful of laughter and tears,
Love and be loved to live life to the full, and gather content from
the years.

Stalwart man and slender maid cease from sweet repining;
Let the palm support the flower by its tendrils climbing.

Life is short and death is long, who knows of its waking?
Love can make the world a song, or torture hearts to breaking.
Love's clarion call is sounding, over both hill and lea;

"Love and be loved to be happy, love and be loved to be free."
Love and be loved to be hopeful, brimful of laughter and tears,
Love and be loved to live life to the full, and gather
content from the years.

The Snoring Queen

She snores away her cares, she snores away her sighs,
She snores the whole night through, when once she's
closed her eyes.
She snores away all worry, she snores away all strife,
She snores at me, she snores at you, she even snores at life.
Of all the first class snorers that I have ever seen,
I bow the knee before her, and I crown her Snoring Queen.

Chorus.

Snoring queen I love you in the daytime when the little
birdies sing,
I love you in the kitchen, you can cook like anything.
I love you when I'm near you, but better out of sight,
I love you in the morning, but I don't love you at night!

Unhappy
When the postman's knock is heard, all my neighbours smile,
He never brings me one from you. I'm grieving all the while;
Perhaps you think I'm strong enough to face my life alone,
But if you only knew how I long for you, my own.

Unhappy when the dawn breaks to herald each new day,
Unhappy when the flowers bloom fragrant, fresh and gay,
Unhappy when I see young lovers strolling on their way,
Unhappy when I ask my God to bless you when I pray,
Unhappy in the summertime, and all the winter through,

Unhappy, so lonely, unhappy without you.
Unhappy without love, dear, unhappy without you.

When the Lightning Flashed

When the lightning flashed and the huge trees crashed,
Along the mountainside,
When the waters whirled and the torrents swirled,
And eddied deep and wide,
I stood in the midst of the storm, my heart a pulsing flame,
I waited in the tempest, but alas, you never came.

When the sun rode high in the clear noon sky,
And little birds did sing,
Buds burst to flowers, the happy hours flew by to the lilt of
spring,
I stood alone in the silence and tenderly breathed your name,
And knew that my heart was broken, for alas, you never came!

See also:
African Nights (Chapter Two)
My Boy (Chapter Five)
The Down and Out Blues (Chapter Five)
The Might Have Been (Chapter Five)

--OOOIIIOOO--

Printed in Dunstable, United Kingdom